Jacket Art - *St. Michael of the Holy Face* (2007):
By Catherine Petrunio, USA

"I feel honored to be a part of this book. I have
four children and five grandchildren. God has
been very good to me. Painting St. Michael and
the Holy Face was another dream. When it came
down to painting the devil, well that was a
challenge, I hope my work will inspire the soul".
– Catherine

Photograph of the author, Gordon Deery:
By Rev. Lawrence Farley, p.d.

The Holy Face of Jesus Christ

The Holy Face of Jesus Christ

Discovery, Journey, Destination

Gordon Deery

Holy Face Association
Montreal, Quebec, Canada H3C 2W9

Scripture passages have been taken from the New Revised Standard Version, Catholic edition. In accordance with the Code of Canon Law Canon 825.1, the New Revised Standard Version, Catholic Edition, has the imprimatur of the National Conference of Catholic Bishops (USA) and the Canadian Conference of Catholic Bishops granted on 12 September 1991 and 15 October 1991 respectively.

Excerpts from the English translation of the Catechism of the Catholic Church for Canada. Copyright © Concacan Inc. – Libreria Editrice Vaticana, 1994, for the English translation in Canada.

Autobiographical Content
Although not a complete autobiography of his life, the events set down in this book are accounts of what happened during a significant portion of the life of the author. The contents, opinions, and statements expressed are as he remembers them for the period described.

DECLARATION
The decree of the Congregation for the Propagation of the Faith A.A.S. 58,1186 (approved by Pope Paul VI on October 14, 1966) states that the **NIHIL OBSTAT** and **IMPRIMATUR** are no longer required on publications that deal with private revelations, provided that they contain nothing contrary to faith and morals. God's servants wish to manifest their unconditional submission to the final and official judgment of the Magisterium of the Church in all matters, including the contents of this book.

Published by Holy Face Association
P.O. Box 100, STN St-Jacques,
Montreal, Québec, Canada
H3C 2W9
www.holyface.com

Cover jacket art: © St. Michael of the Holy Face (2007) by Catherine Petrunio, USA

Printed in Montreal, Québec, Canada
ISBN 978-1-896048-15-4

iv

Table of Contents

DEDICATION

    This book is dedicated to my dear mother and my dear daughter, Christine:

    My mother, Germaine (*now deceased and gone on to receive her eternal reward*) stood by me and worked tirelessly to the end.

    My daughter, Christine, has labored, by my side for over twenty years, to spread the devotion to the Holy Face of Jesus. Her perseverance, support, and guidance have been invaluable for this holy work.

Gordon Deery

ACKNOWLEDGEMENTS

I thank God for having given me a wonderful mother and father; for all the sacrifices they made, and for their love and direction.

Encouragement and inspiration are valuable supports particularly when they come from pillars of faith whose practicality provides strength during moments of difficulty or trial. In this regard, special mention goes to Mgr. André Chimicella (of blessed memory); Rev. Fr. Russell A. Schultz; Rev. Fr. Michael Pintacura; and, Rev. Fr. Joseph di Mauro, S.A.

Catherine Petrunio, whose painting captures the triumph of God who sustains us by the Eucharist and shields us by his divine gaze.

Rev. Lawrence Farley for encouraging me to write this book and then accepting to do the editing.

Countless people – who have, in various ways, helped to promote the Holy Face of our Lord by their witness, volunteer efforts, and financial contributions.

May our Lord and our Blessed Mother continue to reward you on your journey by a share in the many spiritual graces and blessings past, present and those to come.

PROMISES OF OUR LORD JESUS CHRIST
(...to those devoted to His Holy Face)

1.   I will grant them contrition so perfect, that their very sins shall be changed in my sight into jewels of precious gold.

2.   None of these persons shall ever be separated from me.

3.   In offering my Face to my Father, they will appease his anger and they will purchase as with celestial coin, pardon for poor sinners.

4.   I will open my Mouth to plead with my Father to grant all the petitions that they will present to me.

5.   I will illuminate them with my light. I will consume them with my love I will render them fruitful of good works.

6.   They will, as the pious Veronica, wipe my adorable Face outraged by sin, and I will imprint my divine Features in their souls.

7.   At their death, I will renew in them the image of God effaced by sin.

8.   By resemblance to my Face, they will shine more than many others in eternal life and the brilliance of my Face will fill them with joy.

These inestimable promises are drawn from the works of St. Gertrude of St. Mechtilde and from the writings of Sister Maria de Saint-Pierre, a Carmelite, who died at Tours, in the odor of sanctity.

FOREWORD
By Reverend Lawrence N. Farley, p.d, sfo

Long ago God spoke to our ancestors in many and various ways by the prophets, but in these last days he has spoken to us by a Son, whom he appointed heir of all things, through whom he also created the worlds. He is the reflection of God's glory and the exact imprint of God's very being (Heb. 1:1-3).

This brief passage from sacred scripture refers to the appearance of Jesus Christ on the canvas of human history over two thousand years ago. Jesus is the perfect image of the Father – to see him is to see the Father (John 12:45). In 1898, a famous Italian photographer, Secundo Pia, by the authority of the Roman Catholic Church, was given permission to photograph a burial cloth, "The Shroud of Turin", which had long been venerated as being the shroud cloth in which Jesus Christ was buried.

When the extraordinary photograph of the faint ghost-like image on the cloth was taken the plates unexpectedly came out as a "photographic negative", which disclosed the remarkably clear positive features of the body of a crucified man. Many believe the image of this crucified man on the Shroud of Turin to be that of Jesus Christ; and they refer to his facial countenance as "The Holy Face".

The Holy Face image is so tranquil, so majestic, and so compelling that it contradicts human logic: how can the serenity of this countenance co-exist with one of the most extreme and excruciating forms of torture ever devised in the history of the world?

The Holy Face of Jesus Christ is one individual's encounter with Jesus Christ who reveals himself to the great and the small alike. The great ones often pursue the path of details – the particulars of the macro and micro universe of knowledge of arts, letters, and science. The small ones will likewise pursue the path of faith (*less academic perhaps, but nonetheless grandiose*) – where relationship with God tends to be expressed in the profound familial trust between loving children and their devoted parents – it is the familiar piety born of genuine intimacy, whose veritable deeds are the proofs of love.

Over three decades now, my Franciscan brother, Gordon Deery, has shared with me the bits and pieces – like precious gleanings, from the field of his journey of faith. I have always been amazed and edified by these shared-moments. Several years ago, I invited him to share the story underpinning The Holy Face Association in Montreal, Quebec – so others might also derive some benefit.

In Sacred Scripture, there is an incident, which I find fitting to illustrate *The Holy Face of Jesus Christ*. It comes to light...gleaned, as it were, from the 'big picture' of the passion and death of Christ. This Gospel excerpt is the essence of 'the whole truth' about Christ: a nameless woman pours out an expensive ointment on Jesus. It took place on the threshold of the Passover festival of Unleavened Bread (Mark 14:1-9). It might have been overlooked had Jesus not paused to highlight its significance as a beacon for future generations. On account of it, Jesus says,

"...*wherever the Gospel is proclaimed in the whole world, what she has done will be told in memory of her*" (Mark 14:9).

Those who, with their own eyes, saw it happen, judged the nameless woman's "offering" to be wasteful. Yet, what escaped the practical minded, did not escape the penetrating gaze of the Lord: her apparent extravagance symbolizes what Jesus is about to do for the whole world. Just as this woman "breaks open" the exquisite alabaster jar and "pours out" its precious contents over the head of Jesus – in anticipation of his death and burial – so too will Jesus allow his own body "to be broken" by torture and crucifixion and will have the precious ointment of his life-giving blood "poured out" on all human beings destined to die!

There are those who may regard Gordon Deery's journey of self-dedication to promote 'devotion to the love of God' – shining forth on the Holy Face of Jesus Christ – as being too radical! The worldwide scope of this work may intimidate some; and then there's guilt, the pangs of which are felt by those unable to imagine themselves making such sacrifice! Somehow, all of them would miss the mark: love is extravagant; it is extraordinary – it is sacrificial! The anointing of Jesus with oil teaches us that the passion and the self-sacrifice of Jesus upon the wood of the cross... is not primarily about how much Jesus suffered, but rather, it is about how much he loved – love is capable of sacrifice; great love is prepared to make great sacrifice; and perfect love willingly embraces sacrifice with perfection.

Even though you may have had occasion to cross paths with Gordon, you might not have heard the story behind the big picture.

Here is your opportunity! *The Holy Face of Jesus Christ* is about 'the fragrance of love' that is revealed on the face of Christ. It is an everlasting love, which you and I are invited to gaze upon while on earth, not only because we desire the beauty of such fragrant love in the here and now, but also, because it is our destiny to behold it forever in eternity – when the shroud covering the peoples and nations is forever removed (Isaiah 25:7).

You will catch *the substance* of the fragrance of *The Holy Face of Jesus* throughout the pages of sacred scripture:

Psalm 4:6
"There are many who say 'O that we might see some good!' Let the light of your face shine on us, O Lord!"
Psalm 24:5-6
"They will receive blessing from the Lord, and vindication from the God of their salvation. Such is the company of those who seek him, who seek the face of the God of Jacob."
Psalm 27:7-9
"Hear, O Lord, when I cry aloud, be gracious to me and answer me! 'Come,' my heart says, 'Seek his face!' Your face, Lord, do I seek. Do not hide your face from me."
Psalm 31:16
"Let your face shine on your servant; save me in your steadfast love."
Psalm 44:3
"For not by their own sword did they win the land, nor did their own arm give them victory, but your right hand and your arm, and the light of your countenance; for you delighted in them."
Psalm 67:1
"May God be gracious to us and bless us and make his face to shine upon us."

Psalm 80:3
"Restore us O God; let thy face shine, that we may be saved!"

Numbers 6:24-26
"The Lord bless you and keep you; the Lord make his face to shine upon you and be gracious to you; the Lord lift up his countenance upon you and give you peace."

Daniel 9:17
"Now, therefore, O our God, listen to the prayer of your servant and to his supplication and for your own sake, Lord, let your face shine upon your desolated sanctuary."

2 Corinthians 4:6
"Let light shine out of darkness, who has shone in our hearts to give the light of the knowledge of the glory of God in the face of Jesus Christ."

You will catch *the scent* of the fragrance of *The Holy Face of Jesus Christ* from the pages of this book.

Palm Sunday, 2009

Peace be with you.

Chapter 1 - **A Personal Renewal**

1.01 **Regrets**

In 1955, I started my own company in the food distribution business. In the hope of winning large accounts I did a lot of entertaining.

Within 15 years (approximately), I had job-associated stress and was in denial that I had become an alcoholic. I was not living a good life: drinking, staying out late at night and getting up early to go to work.

We had three children - a boy and two girls. When I arrived home, it was usually with a sorrowful heart and a question (in mind) about what was wrong with me – why could I not stop drinking?

On weekends I would not drink so that I would be able to gather enough strength to make it through another week. Throughout the week I was in the company of many who liked to drink. Some of them worked for me and we would find all kinds of excuses to justify our celebrating with a few drinks (that would turn out to be too many).

1.02 **Wake Up Call**

One day in 1971, I went to see my doctor, and was told, "If you don't stop drinking, you are going to die". This was an eye opener, which forced me to take immediate action. If I had not agreed to listen to my doctor, I would not be here today. So, I went to the hospital.

Approximately three weeks later, I received a visit from a man associated with Alcoholics Anonymous – a wonderful organization, which I highly recommend. They helped save my life, and yes, (I must say) my soul.

When I stopped drinking, I asked myself, "What am I doing? What am I accomplishing?" My drinking had hurt so many. Then, it occurred to me that I had forgotten God, and that I had stopped going to Church.

1.03 Hope and Heaven's Gifts

I started going back to Church on Sundays, and then I started to make the Tuesday Devotions to "Our Mother of Perpetual Help".

I had a wonderful experience one morning on my way to the Tuesday Devotions. A man came up to me out of nowhere. I truly believe he was an angel. He had a gift for me. It was a beautiful uniquely made frame – with gold metal, two little doors, and with a cross on the top. When I opened the two little doors, I saw a wonderful picture of "Our Mother of Perpetual Help". This man was dressed as if he was a beggar. "My name is Gordon Deery", I said - and asked him for his name. "Richard Darling", he answered. I have been praying for Richard Darling every morning since; and I treasure this frame, which is one of the best gifts I have ever received.

One Tuesday in 1972, when I was doing the "Mother of Perpetual Help Devotion", the Blessed Mother sent me to the side altar, which had a nice framed picture of the Holy Face of Jesus. I picked up a leaflet, which gave a brief explanation on the *Devotion to the Holy Face* and a Holy Face Medal.

The message was as follows: a holy nun by the name of Mother Maria Pierina was urged, in many visions, by the Blessed Mother (and Jesus Himself), to spread *"Devotion to the Holy Face"*. Devotion was to be in reparation for the many insults Jesus suffered in his passion, (i.e., kissed by Judas, slapped, and spit upon, as well as being dishonored in many ways in the Blessed Sacrament by neglect, sacrileges, and profanations). Mother Pierina was given "a scapular", which on one side bore a replica of the Holy Face of Jesus and the inscription: *"May, O Lord, the light of Thy countenance shine upon us"* (Ps. 80:3). The reverse side bore a radiant host with the words: *"Stay with us O Lord"* (Luke 24:29)

Because this took place during the Second World War, Mother Pierina had medals made instead of scapulars, for which our Blessed Mother subsequently confirmed as having the same promises as the scapular. Our Blessed Mother told her that the medal is a weapon for defense, a shield for courage, and a token of love and mercy, which her Divine Son wished to give the world in these troubled days of lust and hatred for God and for his Church. She said that devilish snares have been set to rob the hearts of men, of their faith, while evil spreads the world over; that genuine apostles are few; and that a divine remedy to all these evils is the adorable face of her son, Jesus.

Whoever wears this medal, and if possible, pays a weekly visit to the Blessed Sacrament on Tuesday, in a spirit of reparation for the outrages received by the Holy Face of our Blessed Savior during his passion, and those bestowed on him every day in the Sacrament of His Divine love, will be granted the gift of a strong faith and the grace to come to its defense, conquering, if need be, all interior and exterior difficulties. They are also promised a happy death with special assistance from Jesus himself.

What a treasure! How can anyone refuse such love – and such awesome promises? I did not hesitate to make a phone call, and I made an appointment to meet this nun in order to find out more about the message.

The very next day was the day I made the most important move in my life! It was the day when the Holy Face Medal was placed around my neck, and it was then that I truly gave my life to God until the day when I would die. I said to our Lord, "I no longer wish to run my life. Until now, I have done so, and made a mess of it. Through our Blessed Mother I ask you to please take over my life".

I continued to go to A.A. meetings twice a week, and was smoking a package of cigarettes each day. I also had another bad habit that I presumed would remain with me until my death. However, I had not realized the power of the Holy Face Medal and its tremendous promises.

1.04 **A Vocal Multitude**

One day, when I was challenged by a bad habit, all of a sudden, there came to me a great multitude of voices (not of this world)! I could sense they were souls from purgatory. And they seemed to be working hard to make sure that I heard them. The voices were full of love, and concern for me. All they said and kept repeating was one word: "No, No, No"!

This experience was so impressive that not only did the bad habit stop, but I no longer needed to attend anymore A.A. meetings, for I knew without a shadow of a doubt, that drinking for me, was the influence of the devil - for when I drank, I lost my will to resist. Whatever takes away your will to resist is evil, and causes one to fall into greater temptation and eventually – sin, whether it is alcohol or drugs, etc. I knew if someone offered me an alcoholic drink, the devil was behind the scene trying to make me fall. I also stopped smoking.

At that time, I attended the weekly "Tuesday Devotions" of our *Mother of Perpetual Help*. It was comforting to make the Tuesday's of reparation at St. Patrick's Basilica, in Montreal, Canada. As usual, my first stop was to bring flowers for our Blessed Mother and for the altar of the Holy Face of Jesus. Every time I went into the Church, the very first prayer said was for the intentions of the Pope, then an Our Father, a Hail Mary, and a Glory Be, in front of the Blessed Sacrament. Then I would go see our Blessed Mother, for she was the one who was running my life; of course, she would always send me to her Beloved Son Jesus, Son of the Living God.

1.05 **Pulsing Eyes**

When she sent me to Jesus, I had the feeling it was to go to his most Holy Face - the image on the Holy Shroud.

So, down I went to the "St. Joseph Altar", where the beautiful Holy Face picture was enshrined; but to my amazement, the Holy Face of Jesus became alive: the eyes opened and the Holy Face was pulsating. Something was wrong - this could not be! I stayed for about thirty minutes to see if it would stop, but it never did, so I thought maybe something was wrong with me, and I left.

That night, all I thought about was what had happened, and I prayed asking our Lord, what was happening? The next morning, I went to see the Holy Face of Jesus again. I was curious to see what would happen. Again, the Holy Face was pulsating and the eyes of Jesus were looking at me. I asked a lady who was close to me if she saw the Holy Face of Jesus, with his eyes open, and pulsating. She gave me a look as if to say, "You belong in a nut house", so I knew she could not see it. As I was deeply affected by this experience, I kept Jesus company for a long time but still hesitated to accept what was happening.

That night, I was very restless and asked many questions about why this was happening. Why was I the only one who saw this? Why was our Lord showing me this sign?

For a third morning, I returned to the church, and after my visit to our dear Blessed Mother, I made my way to the Holy Face of Jesus, and once again it was pulsating and the eyes, so full of love, were looking straight at me.

I felt such a feeling of love, that I knelt down, and like St. Thomas, I said *"My Lord and My God"* (John 20:28), and I burst into tears - of love, of so much joy, and of sorrow - for being such a great sinner, because I was so sorry for all the times I had hurt Jesus.

I stayed there for a very long time in a spirit of penitential love and sorrow.

As much as I can remember, one of my first acts was to go and make a good confession at the Franciscan Monastery, on Dorchester Boulevard. Through the grace of God, I was growing very fast in faith, love, and hope.

1.06 **The Pilgrimage**

Shortly afterwards, I was brought to the Church of Our Lady of Lourdes by my mother and father, who had a Mass offered for me. A couple of weeks after this Mass, I had a great desire to go to Jerusalem to see the Holy Face of Jesus, and then, to Italy, Rome, and Assisi - so off we went.

In 1973, when in Jerusalem, we went to Bethlehem, Nazareth, and to many different places where our Lord walked to the Garden of Gethsemane, plus Calvary where our Lord was Crucified, the tomb where he was buried, and so many other holy sites. During all this time, I was searching for the Holy Face of Jesus, and did not see it, to my great disappointment. His most Holy Face was nowhere to be found!

As long as I live, my trip to the Holy Land will never be forgotten. There was so much to be seen, and in such a short time; it was difficult to take it all in. It was awesome! Prayers being said 24 hours a day... certainly helps to open one's eyes.

Then, on to Rome where of course, again, there was so much to see: the Vatican and so many other beautiful Shrines; and churches, with such a great history. However no matter how much I searched, I could not find the Holy Face of Jesus anywhere. How could this be? What was the matter with everyone? Then I said to myself surely it would be in Assisi, after all, St. Francis used to bless all his brothers and sisters with the blessing of the Holy Face from the Book of Numbers (6:22-27).

Assisi, what a Holy City it is. Even on the way there, you could actually feel a peace come upon you! Truly, it was very special for me! It was a very prayerful time, and I saw many of the places where St. Francis used to pray. Still I could not find the image of the Holy Face of Jesus.

1.07 **Cleansing Waters**

Now, time came for me to return home, but something seemed to be calling me to go to Lourdes, so I decided to stay there three days, where I did much praying, bombarding Heaven with my prayers, my sighs, and my disappointments. How sad no one seemed to display the Holy Face of Jesus. Yet I was so pleased to be at this shrine of our Lady.

On my last day in Lourdes, I decided that I might as well go bathe in the waters from the spring where so many had been cured. While waiting in line, one man who worked there asked me to help him to place all the sick people in the water. After we were finished, I said to myself "He won't ask me to go in the water because I am all wet" but no, he told me to be prepared to go into the water.

When I finally went into the water, it was so very cold! He then took my head, and pushed me under the water before I had a chance to take a breath! When my head came up out of the water, I opened my mouth to take a breath and he took a glass of the water and placed it on my mouth to drink it. Then I said to myself "Oh my heavens, all those germs"!

I had read about the water, however, and even though there are many, many germs, they are all dead. When you come out of the water, you seem to be dry. I don't know why they even bothered to give me a towel.

The man I had helped thanked me and asked me to follow him into his office. It was here, in this place, for the first time on my pilgrim journey, that I saw the image of the Holy Face of Jesus. The man then gave me a red rose, which I knew came from my dear Blessed Mother. I was so pleased.

1.08 **The Master's Question**

It was my last night in Lourdes. I was sleeping. At approximately one o'clock in the morning, I woke up. I sensed that Jesus himself was in the room! I felt so unworthy! Our Lord spoke to me, and (make no mistake) when our Lord speaks to you, even though he is very gentle, his voice is full of authority. You listen very carefully and with the greatest of respect.

Our Lord said to me, "You took a long time to wake up". His few words carried great meaning. I was 43 years old then – and I have no answer for this, but he was telling me, that I had to do more than many others to make up for lost time. Our Lord asked me, "Do you think that you can do it"?"

What did he mean by this? Was he asking me to persevere? I had no idea what he meant, but I had to answer. If I say yes, he will say I am far from being humble. If I say no, then I lack love and faith. So I answered after what seemed to me to be a very long delay, "Yes, but only with the help of my Blessed Mother". Our Lord seemed pleased with the answer and left.

If you were to ask me what our Lord looked like, my answer would be that I did not feel worthy to gaze upon his Holy Face. If our Lord were to come today to see me, I would definitely look at Him, for I love him too much not to look upon his Holy Face. The next morning, in prayer, our Lord told me, "You had a lot of problems to find my Holy Face – but one day it will be throughout the world". I had made a wonderful pilgrimage, and it was now time to return home.

Our Lord and Blessed Mother had shown me that our Lord's most Holy Face was not being venerated. People just did not realize the tremendous gift that our Heavenly Father has sent to a suffering world - the actual image of the MOST HOLY FACE OF HIS BELOVED SON, JESUS.

Through the Holy Face of Jesus one can overcome all the problems in the world, if one really and truly wishes to accept Jesus, *"Lord show us your Face and we shall be saved"* (Psalm 80:3).

1.09 **The Master's Meaning**

I returned to Montreal, and went back to my business. At that time, I owned two homes (fully paid for). Both homes were picture-perfect, and beautifully furnished by interior decorators. One home was in a good district called St. Bruno, while the other was truly beautiful in the country, on Orford Lake, and had a boathouse with five boats. My wife and I each had our own cars: one, a Mark 3 - the other, a Mustang convertible.

Once back in Montreal, I went to St. Patrick's Basilica on Tuesday. As I walked into the Church, my feet felt as though they were glued to the floor. I could go no further, but then all of a sudden, I felt the Holy Spirit come very gently from the top of my head to the tips of my toes. I felt a power – a tingling, very, very gentle (not of this world) - and I felt like Mary

Madeleine, as if many evil spirits had been taken away from me!

After the Mass, I just did not want to leave; it was so very peaceful. While I was sitting quietly in the pew, this little old lady came up to me; gave me a small, used book; and said, "I have had this book for 25 years but now I want you to have it". So, I took the little book. It was so small that it took no more than 10 minutes to read.

In reading the book, it said very clearly: "Go and close your business". Is this what our Lord meant when he said, "Do you think you can do it"?

1.10 **A Matter of Trust**

The next week I started to get prepared to close the business. The news certainly was not taken well by many people. I had to try to be gentle, and fair with everyone, and of course with the employees. It must have taken about three months to close the business.

There were still loose ends to tie up; however, when this had been done, our Lord showed me that I had to sell my two homes, which I did.

Then, I was told that I was to get rid of my car, which I also did. And then, our Lord said I should get rid of all my money! I did this, of course, but I kept about $5,000.00 in case of emergency.

These changes affected our marriage. Understandably, these new developments were not fully comprehended or accepted by my wife at the time. Today, she is helping to spread the devotion.

When I returned to the church on Tuesday, I felt that I had done what our Lord had asked, so I opened the Holy Bible three times, as St. Francis used to do. The first time it said, "Get rid of your money". I then opened it a second and third time. It said the same thing! So, no more time was wasted. I got rid of the $5.000.00.

Now I had nothing - not one cent to my name, no home, no business, and no job. By this time, I was sleeping on a lawn chair, in an apartment, where the rent had been paid for approximately two more weeks. I did not even have one washcloth!

I was wondering if I had done what our Lord had asked me to do. I returned to the church.

When I knelt to pray our Lord told me, "Before, you were putting your trust in the $5,000.00 and now you are putting your trust in me. Now I will take over" (This was in 1974).

Chapter 2 – **The Narrow Path**

2.01 **Trials and Discernment**

We know that to follow in our Lord's footsteps means we too must face trials and obstacles.

Remember what Simeon said to our Blessed Mother at the presentation of Jesus to our Heavenly Father, "*He will be a sign that will be rejected by many, and a sword will piece your own heart too*" (Luke 2:35). This rejection is happening in our days.

While attempting to follow the Lord, I went to meet the Bishop in order to begin training to become a deacon. A month later, a priest told me I could not be a deacon without the support of my wife.

After hearing I could not be a deacon I became very sad, and went to the Franciscan Monastery. There was a nun at the desk, strange, because there is usually a brother or porter at the desk to meet people.

The nun noticed I was sad, and she said, "Why are you so sad"? I told her because I was told I could not become a deacon, but she answered, "Our Lord has something else for you to do; He does not want you to be a deacon".

About one week later, a priest asked if I could go to a Bible class he was having, so I went. However, just when the class was about to begin, a Franciscan nun arrived (not the same nun I had met before). I had never seen this nun before. She looked at me, and said in front of everyone present, "What are you doing here? You are not supposed to be here." Now I was really mixed up! What is happening to me? What does our Lord want me to do?

2.02 **My Vocation**

I was shown that I should open the "Holy Face Association". This was our Lord's association; it is consecrated to The Holy Family - Jesus, Mary, and Joseph.

I knew, without any doubt that this is why I was born. My God-given responsibility was to spread devotion to the Most Holy Face of Jesus throughout the world, until the day I die. This is the reason I am on earth.

Our Lord and Blessed Mother had shown me how very few truly loved Jesus.

Our Heavenly Father has sent to modern society, what prophets had desired to see and could not, the actual most Holy Face of his Beloved Son, Jesus.

2.03 **Starting Over**

My first priority now was to find a job, so I could at least pay rent and buy some food. One of my friends was working for a large meat packer and food distributor. I asked him to help me meet his boss, whom I knew very well myself.

At the meeting, when the president of the company, Mr. Guy Lauzon (senior) learned that I desperately needed a job, he told me, "I cannot afford you"! I was told that he had many employees, approximately 600. He knew how much money I used to make, but I told him I was not the same man, and that I would work for a lot less, on the condition I would work directly under him, to which he agreed.

My first move was to get a good spiritual director and I chose a Franciscan priest, Fr. Dieu Donné Massée. I then joined the Third Order of St. Francis (now known as The Secular Franciscan Order) and took the name Dismas (the good thief). I figured if Jesus would save the good thief, why not me? My mother and fourteen-year-old daughter also joined the Third Order of St Francis.

Then to my surprise, a few months after joining the Third Order, they voted me Minister Prefect. To me, this was a great honor, but of course, also a great responsibility.

When one joins a Religious Order as a layperson, one promises to live according to a "Rule of Life" in accordance with the approved constitutions and the particular charism of that order.

One would be "in the world", but would not live as though they were "of the world". I then made a vow of celibacy to our Lord and Blessed Mother, and I have kept this promise for over 36 years.

Now, I had to be able to get around, so I bought a second hand car for $500.00 ($100.00 down, and $100.00 financing per month). It was a Datsun, a small car with one major defect - it backfired with a very, very loud "bang"! I felt so sorry when it did this, because in the rear view mirror, I could see people so upset, they were shaking their fists at me.

At about the same time all this was happening, my father passed away. My mother, bless her heart, asked to live with me. I was pleased, because it gave me much pleasure to be able to take care of her. My mother sold her home, and gave me $5,000.00 to start up the Holy Face Association. She told me she did this, because I helped to pay their bills when my father was sick.

Before I started the Holy Face Association, I made sure that I had the permission of Monsignor Leonard Crowley, Auxiliary Bishop of the Diocese of Montreal, Quebec, Canada, because I knew that the Holy Face Association must at all times be in total obedience to the Holy Roman Catholic Church. It was, and has been repeatedly consecrated to Jesus, Mary, and Joseph. It is Our Lord's Association, through the intercession of our Blessed Mother and St. Joseph.

Whenever I wanted to discern if I should let a person work with the Association, or if I should listen to a religious, I would always ask three questions:

1- Do you believe in the "Infallibility of the Pope"?

2- Do you believe in the "Immaculate Conception"?

3- Do you believe in the "Assumption of our Blessed Mother (body and soul) into Heaven"?

If they said "no" to even one of these questions, I would be cautious with these people.

My mother and I began to spread the Holy Face of Jesus medals and prayer leaflets throughout the world. We were shown the medals should be freely given, one per person. It is the most simple of devotions. Moreover, what can be more natural than "to seek the face of the one you love"? Surely, you don't hide the face of your loved one! As the medals are free, who can have an excuse that he or she could not afford it?

2.04 Devilish Attacks

But, the devil was not happy with us! One day, I was on the second floor of a building, which was under construction. Accidentally, someone bumped into me and I fell over backwards (head first) from the second floor to the main floor and landed on my back on the cement floor. Yet, as I was falling, I felt tremendous peace. I was unhurt but my Holy Face medal had a small dent. Jesus saved me!

In our apartment, we had all the Holy Face devotional material. Because we are proud of Jesus, we had placed a picture of his Holy Face on our front door (we must boldly witness to Jesus who paid the debt of our sins out of love for us). Therefore, we must always take pride in showing others Jesus, to whom we belong - our Lord and our God!

Our Lord said that whoever is ashamed of him, he will likewise be ashamed of in the presence of his heavenly Father (Matthew 10:33).

One day there was a huge fire in our apartment building. The flames were shooting out from the roof. Three fire stations responded, and of course, we had to leave. The next morning, we went back to see what damage had been done. As we walked into the building, the tenants were downstairs. The neighbors in front of us, above us, and, below us said, "Don't bother going to your apartment, we have lost everything due to the smoke and water damage".

We walked up to our apartment. As usual, the Holy Face of Jesus was still on our front door. We opened the door, expecting the worst, but it was as if we were under the protection of the gaze of Jesus. There was no fire damage, no water, and no smell of smoke.

We called the movers, asked them to bring empty boxes, packed up everything, and dropped it into the moving truck from the second balcony. When all was moved, we took the Holy Face picture off the front door, and immediately a strong scent of smoke came into our apartment. Also, much water gushed into the apartment. It is as if our Lord said that 'those of you, who honor me, I will protect in a special manner'.

2.05 **Dedication and Success**

I knew it would be hard work to find customers and open up new accounts for the company president (it was only right for me to earn my wages). For the first six months, at least four days a week, I worked hard to get large accounts and through the grace of God, my sales skyrocketed with some very large accounts. Some of my old contacts were placed in high positions where they were able to help me to secure large orders.

My mother, daughter, and others, who donated their time to help Jesus, worked with me on the Holy Face of Jesus every weekend. Here, I must give special mention to Suzanne and Frank Mancuso, my Franciscan sister and brother, without whom we could not have done it.

2.06 Blessings Beyond Boundaries

I had a habit every morning when I got up, after I was dressed. I would take "Holy Water", make "the Sign of the Cross", and then on my forehead I would trace the initials "I.N.R.I", while saying "Jesus, king of the Jews, protect me and my family during the day". At night, I would do the same, but say, "protect me and my family" throughout the night, while sprinkling "Holy Water" on my bed. One night, my mother and my daughter had gone to bed. Their bedroom door was closed. My bedroom door was also closed. And as was my custom, I finished saying the little prayer, and sprinkled "holy water". My daughter immediately called out to me and then knocked on my door. She said that I had just thrown "holy water" on her! She said as soon as the water touched her, she knew without a shadow of a doubt, that it was "holy water". My mother's reaction was to look up at the ceiling in her room to see where it was leaking. But it was neither leaking nor raining! Our Lord was showing me that he was pleased with this prayer.

2.07 **Holy Face Illuminations**

One day, in prayer, it came to me that I should try and place a framed picture of the Holy Face of Jesus in different churches throughout the western hemisphere. It came to me that I should make a wood box frame for the Holy Face of Jesus, which would be illuminated from behind the picture by a light placed within the box frame. In this way, every detail of the Holy Face of Jesus would show up clearly, even if one were to look at the Holy Face picture from a distance of a hundred feet away.

The first lighted box frames were made of wood and were very pleasing to look at. After I had placed these frames in different churches, I realized that I had omitted installing a pane of glass (as a heat barrier) at the back of the frame – causing the picture to wrinkle due to the heat from the bulbs. So I returned to the churches, which housed the first illuminated frames. At the first church, I returned to, I spoke with the priest and was told that he had tolerated the Holy Face for a short period of time and then had placed it in the basement. I was shocked when he said this! I knelt down, asked for his blessing, and then left without even asking for the frame.

Then I told Jesus "Who am I to have such an honor as to place your Holy Face in churches"? Then, I said if I don't get a sign that I should continue to do this, I would stop placing his picture in churches. The next day, I went to another church where the Holy Face was placed. When I walked into the church, the priest was celebrating Mass. To my knowledge, I did not know this priest.

I decided to wait until after the Mass to ask the priest for permission to fix the Holy Face frame. I was pleased to see that the Holy Face picture was placed next to the Blessed Sacrament, and was lit up. After Mass, I went to see the priest, and there were many ladies also waiting to see him.

Again, I decided to wait until all the ladies had finished speaking with the priest. But to my surprise, he walked past those ladies and came directly over to me, put his two arms around my neck and said, "Gordon Deery, it has been exactly one year today since you placed the Holy Face of Jesus in the church, and all we have had is graces and blessings! Thank you, thank you, thank you"!

And I said to Jesus, "Thank you for showing me that I should continue to place the Holy Face frames in different churches". How wonderful it was to see a priest who had such a great love for Jesus and God's children!

2.08 God's Inspirations

Through the grace of God, I continued to place the Holy Face of Jesus pictures in many cathedrals, basilicas, and churches.

One day, I went to a cathedral and met the bishop. He asked to have the Holy Face picture placed in the cathedral, on one side of the statue of Saint Thérèse de Lisieux. Then he made a comment:

"Wouldn't it be nice if there was another frame of the infant Jesus on the other side of the statue"? I went and purchased a beautiful picture of the infant Jesus and put it in a lighted box frame that matched the other one and placed it on the other side of the statue, so that we now had Saint Thérèse de Lisieux and of the Holy Face. Again, a small inspiration (which I acted on) suggested that I put two small boxes on the marble rail - one containing the Holy Face prayer leaflets in French and the other Holy Face prayer leaflets in English.

When I returned about a week later to make sure that everything was okay, someone had taken the two boxes that had the English and French leaflets away! So I went back, bought two more boxes, fixed them up nicely and placed them back on the railing with some tape underneath so that they would not fall off. I figured they would stay there.

I returned one week later, and the boxes were removed again so I went back to the store, bought another two boxes, fixed them up nicely once again, put the tape underneath it again and placed it on the marble railing. All of a sudden, I heard a voice behind me; it was the bishop! He said, "Oh it's you! You're like Saint Francis! We throw you out the front door and you come in by the side door"! He laughed, and those boxes are still there until this very day!

My mother loved to set a good table. When a priest came over for supper, the table would be beautiful, with sterling silver candleholders, etc. We had many priests and nuns who used to come to our home - sometimes from as far away as California, and even the Philippines! When they had finished eating, I would clear the dining room table, and then place all the wood on the table that I needed to make more frames. I would start sawing and hammering and eventually drill the lighted box frames. This, of course, would upset my mother, and she used to say, "Oh my table! Oh my table", because she used to enjoy having it nicely decorated. After a few weeks, however, she gave up and laughingly said, "Oh, what's the use"?

Of course, my devotion to the Holy Face of Jesus continued to grow daily. When I came back from Lourdes, I remembered how our Lord had told me that I had taken such a long time to wake up, so I started to make up for lost time. I would go to two masses every morning, serving the seven o'clock mass at the cathedral - and then the eight o' clock mass at Saint Patrick's Basilica, no matter what the weather was like.

I am continuing to grow in the love of Jesus. What a gift we have received from our Heavenly Father! If only souls realized what they have been given, they would beg for this gift, which has been reserved for this modern generation. I received the gift of tears, and no matter what, I could not stop crying for weeks.

When I was in Church one day to keep our Lord company and to make reparation for all those poor souls who don't love Jesus, our Lord showed me, how much love there is in heaven. Oh my, if one were to gather up all the love in the world from the beginning of time, it would not even be enough to fill a tiny thimble when compared to the love in heaven.

2.09 **A Mother's Sacrifice**

I had a keen awareness of my faults, and a deep sorrow for them. My whole life was Jesus, and I had a burning desire for the conversion of souls, which I found were so precious in the eyes of God.

My whole life was about love and reparation, about thanksgiving and the tremendous importance of bringing souls back to God through this devotion to the most Holy Face of Jesus, Son of the living God. I felt our Blessed Mother was always next to me, helping me in this God-given work.

I often asked myself, "Why me"? I am so unworthy to have been given the tremendous grace to work with the Holy Face of Jesus. One day, I believe the answer came to me. My mother told me, "When I was a young girl, about 14 years old, I used to get an allowance of 25 cents a week. Then, I would go to the Church of Our Lady of Lourdes. On the roof of the Church was a statue of Our Lady of Lourdes and on her head was a crown with twelve little lights that light up at night that could be seen from far away.

My mother mentioned that it cost 25 cents a week to keep those lights lit – and that she used to give her allowance to pay to keep the lights lit. All she asked for in return from our Blessed Mother was that when she married and had a son, she hoped that he would "do something special for God".

What a treasure to have a mother who loves Jesus and His wonderful Mother!

2.10 **Mr. Lauzon's Contributions**

By now, I was so busy with the Holy Face Association that I hardly had time to do my other work for Mr. Lauzon. Six days a week for the Holy Face - and one for Mr. Lauzon. When I used to walk into the office, Mr. Lauzon would say, "Are you busy Gordon"? I would reply "yes" (but with the Holy Face of Jesus). Then I got worried, for I figured my sales would be very bad - but someone told me, "I don't know what you did, but you have the highest sales of the week".

So, our Lord was taking care of me, along with Saint Joseph the worker. By this time, we had Holy Face leaflets being distributed throughout the world in large quantities. We were getting leaflets printed by the hundreds of thousands. Mr. Lauzon donated $20,000 to the Holy Face Association, which of course, was a great help.

When he passed away, I can only imagine how he beheld the Holy Face of Jesus, taking with him the blessings of wiping away the spittle from the Face of Jesus and helping many to return to Jesus, in a spirit of love and reparation.

Those who contribute financially to God's work receive blessings in this life and reward in the next. They have a share in God's work.

Chapter 3 - **Sowers Of Seed**

3.01 **Feeding the Children**

My spiritual director passed away; he was a wonderful holy priest, who helped me to stay on a straight path to Heaven. He will always be in my daily prayers.

In 1976, my new spiritual director was Father Ralph Dunn, a humble Franciscan priest. Father Ralph used to go to different schools to teach the high school children. One day, Father asked me if I would be interested in talking to the children about the Holy Face, the Holy Shroud and about the devotion to our Blessed Mother. Therefore, I bought what was necessary to be able to do a good job of teaching, for you had to show pictures (project them on the wall) in order for them to understand. I went to the U.S. where we were given different articles, which would help us to better spread the word of God. We also purchased many slides, etc., on our Blessed Mother's apparitions, the Acts of the Apostles, the Holy Shroud details, plus many more slides on the lives of Saints

I was with my mother, when we brought all these Spiritual treasures back into Canada, but we certainly did not expect what happened at the border. A female inspector seemed to lose control. She ran back and forth with her arms in the air and before we knew it two male border guards, as well as the female guard, had me placed in a room and told my mother who was outside, "don't move". They searched me, made me empty all my pockets, and wallet.

They were very upset, so I said to them, "Why are you so upset"? If you wish, we will give you whatever we have, on condition it will be used to help save souls! They also made my mother empty her purse (she was such a gentle soul). She asked me, "What is wrong with these people?" I whispered in her ear, "I believe the devil is not pleased with what we are doing. I truly think that through the grace of God many of his children will return to Jesus, by seeing what we have in this car". After many hours, they finally let us go, and charged us $100.00. It was a small price to pay to save souls.

For many years, the devotion was shared with students in their classrooms. I remember in one of the showings there were approximately eighty children. I had prepared a table where we offered the children rosaries, Holy Face medals with instructions on the different devotions. Father Ralph was sitting in the corner. He came to see me and mentioned that he heard the teachers say, "When the gang comes in, they will laugh him (meaning me) out of the classroom". I replied, "I am here with my hands, but it is the Blessed Mother who is here teaching her children".

After I had spoken to the children about the Holy Face of Jesus and Our Blessed Mother, the first ones who came to get the medals, etc., were "the gang". Father Ralph then heard the teachers say, "We were wrong, and we should be teaching the children more about God".

Another day, when I was in a classroom, I spoke to the students about drugs and told them not to follow the kids who take drugs, for they were the weak ones. The strong ones were those who refused to take drugs - the ones who run their own lives. The teacher was surprised that I had spoken about drugs only in that class, for it was the class where a gang was selling drugs.

The gang members were so mad at me that they threw the Holy Face pictures on the floor. After the talk, though, many children came up to me, thanking me for warning them.

One day Father Ralph Dunn and I went for lunch in a restaurant. The waitress who served us was one of the students who listened to the talks about the Holy Shroud, and Holy Face medal. Pointing to me, Father asked her, "Do you remember this man?" She said no! He then said, "He is the one who spoke about the Holy Shroud and Holy Face medal. Oh! She said, "I will never forget that, for as long as I live". This is what's important. This shows the importance of proclaiming Jesus.

Father David Gourlay was also involved with many schools in the Montreal area. He was very kind and had a great devotion to the most Holy Face of Jesus. We visited many of these schools for years, but the one that comes to mind is a grade school for young children. When we asked if they attended Sunday Mass, most said they had not! I explained to them the tremendous importance of Sunday mass, and said, "I would like to tell you a true story about a young nine or ten year old boy who attended Sunday Mass at the Franciscan Church. This boy would always come dressed in a nice suit with a shirt and a tie. He was always alone, and sat in the first row, and listened attentively to the priest. When he received communion on his tongue, his hands joined together, he would kneel down and talk to Jesus. Within two months, this same boy came to church holding his mother's hand. But this time he and his mom sat in the last row of the church. Approximately two months later, the same boy came to church holding hands with his father and mother. Perhaps others thought the parents were bringing their son to church, but it was actually the little boy bringing his mother and father back to church and back to God through his prayers. "... *a little child shall lead them*" (Isaiah 11:6).

I made sure they received Holy Face pictures and medals, etc., and told them whenever they had problems they should turn to God and to our Blessed Mother to receive help. They returned home full of zeal for Jesus.

I once received a letter from a young man. He wanted to thank me. He had been a student in one of the schools where I had given a talk. He said due to that talk, he was now a priest. Thank you, Jesus, for being such a wonderful God. "*He will receive blessing from the Lord, and vindication from the God of his salvation. Such is the generation of those who seek him, who seek the face of the God of Jacob*" (Psalm 24:5-6).

3.02 Scapular Blessings

I would like to share another story with you. One of my daughters opened a religious, non-profit organization called "Scapular Center". In total, she made fourteen different kinds of cloth scapulars. I was visiting different people in retirement homes and hospitals. In one of the hospitals, a Muslim asked me if I could help him to become a Canadian citizen. Through the grace of God, I was able to do so. He was so pleased, and he asked what he could do for me. This man had muscular dystrophy. I told him, "Nothing".

I was pleased to be of help, but he insisted, so I said, "For one week, wear the Brown Scapular of Our Lady of Mount Carmel, and the Holy Face medal". When the week was up, I went back to see him, and as soon as he saw me, he said, "When I put the scapular and the Holy Face medal on I felt a power come over me. I want to become a Catholic". My spiritual director, who was a Franciscan priest, Father Justin Bellrose, was the Catholic priest at the same Hospital, so he started teaching this man the Catholic Faith.

After about three weeks when I was visiting this man, the Holy Spirit inspired me, and I told the man, "I must warn you, you will be tested very soon. A man will come to see you, he will sit in this corner chair and will tell you to take off that scapular, saying 'Look, I am a Catholic and I don't wear one, so take it off'. However, this will be a test. You must choose whether you want the Blessed Mother, or human respect. You have free will".

When I returned to visit him the week after, I could actually feel a black curtain in front of me. When he saw me, he said, "I don't want to become a Catholic any more". I asked him what had happened.

He said, "A man came to see me, sat in that chair in the corner and told me that he was a Catholic and that I should not wear the scapular, saying that I should 'take that thing off', and I did. I responded to him, "Humble yourself, and put it back on". He refused and lost all the graces that had been given to him.

One day, my daughter was going to see some relatives. I told her they would do all in their power to have her take off the scapular, because I believe one is always tested to see if one is worthy to wear this scapular of the Blessed Mother. Sure enough, they tried everything to have her remove this scapular, which says right on it, "Those who wear this scapular shall not suffer eternal fire". The scapular is approximately 1 x 1.5 inches. Why would a person make so much noise about such a small piece of cloth? My daughter passed the test, and she and her son are both wearing the brown scapular every day; with the Holy Face medal attached.

3.03 **Pilgrimage to Italy**

Around 1978, the Holy Shroud was being shown in Turin, Italy. The Blue Army with John Haffert had a Pilgrimage going to Turin, St. Michael's Cave, Padre Pio, Our Lady of Fatima, St. Anthony, the Holy House of Loreto, etc. I really wanted to go on that trip. When I called, they said it was totally booked, with a long waiting list. I prayed to the Holy Face of Jesus, and our Blessed Mother to get me on that pilgrimage. Within approximately one week, I received a phone call, saying that they had room for me.

It was a tremendous and prayerful pilgrimage. And seeing the actual "Holy Shroud", was a great honor! When we went to see Padre Pio's tomb, and as I passed in front of his confessional, I had a strong smell of the "stigmata". I prayed to Padre Pio that he would come to hear my confession.

Padre Pio, the stigmatized Capuchin of Petrelcina, Italy, sent the pilgrims who visited him to Turin saying: "Go to Turin to see that holy picture, which is the true likeness of the Face of Jesus in Paradise". That same Holy Face picture has to be held in great respect and veneration on account of its merit. This is the holy image of the Lord's likeness that will be a blessing for Turin and Italy.

We visited many shrines. I don't remember all of them but I will mention those that I do. We went to see the Holy Shroud in Turin. What an impression it made on us; the actual burial cloth of Jesus, which shows all the terrible sufferings he endured for our sins! It is the Holy Face that endured all the slaps blows, spits, and laughter. Our Lord was treated like a mock king. The Holy Shroud shows all the marks of the scourging, the blood, and water from the wounds, and his heart being pierced by a lance.

In Turin we saw the Shrine in honor of St. John Bosco. It was a very beautiful Shrine with a lovely picture of the Blessed Mother on the ceiling of the shrine, and a story all of its own. The cave of St. Michael was also very impressive, with special promises attached to one's visit. I highly recommend it.

Our last stop was the Shrine of Our Lady of Fatima. It is always very special, and a great honor to visit one of our Blessed Mother's shrine. You can never say enough about the graces one receives for doing so. After all, we are her children, and she is so pleased when we go out of our way to visit with her, and thank her for everything she does for us; for her daily intercession on our behalf with Jesus, her precious Son, our Lord, and our God.

On my return to Montreal, as usual after a pilgrimage, I was in total peace, but back to work. By this time, the Holy Face Association was truly very busy and taking a lot more time in order to answer correspondence from all over the world. One could see that it was our Lord, his Blessed Mother, and St. Joseph who were running this Association. I was using my hands, but our Lord was bringing and sending souls to the Association.

3.04 Padre's Visit

I had been back home for approximately two months. I had a good habit of going to confession about once a week at the Franciscan Monastery where I went to daily Mass. However, one Saturday (our Lady's first Saturday), I decided to go to St. Joseph's Oratory. When I entered the church I proceeded to go to confession where they always had it in the far corner of the Church - but I was shown, by a strong interior feeling, "No! Sit down in a pew and wait", which I did. Shortly afterwards, I saw a Franciscan friar dressed in his habit with the hood over his head. He went into the middle confessional, which I had never seen used before. I was shown it was Padre Pio

1 Peter 3:11

Seek peace & follow after it
spend life not on human
desire but on the Will of God.
let love for one another
be intense - Peter 4:8
because love covers a multi-
Be hospitable without complains

July 6 — ferst day
weght lose

1, always have
diet book in seght

2. buy fresh, not
canned, if possible

3. have snacks in freg
avaelable

4. look up nutriter
low cal menus +
for Sea Ranch

5. menuru / deisk

6. pray dauly — Novena
weight loset

7. bikes? Twice a week

won over — without a word ... by
reverant + chaste behavor

gentle + calm disposition
keep tongue from evl + lips from
speaking delag

who had heard my plea to come and hear my confession.

I went into the confessional so awed that I could hardly believe this great grace. Padre Pio heard my confession, and when I was finished he said, "What about your sins against charity"? I answered, "I don't have any sins against charity". But then, all of a sudden, a tremendous sorrow came upon me and I said, "Of course I have sins against charity", and burst into many tears of sorrow, after which he gave me absolution.

Then he told me "Please tell the man who is waiting to come to confession to go to the corner confessional". He told me this to show that he had come just for me. I watched him when he left the confessional and he still wore the hood, which hid his face, and he shuffled slowly to the corner and disappeared. How good our Lord is! Sometimes the Lord gives us extraordinary and singular graces to deepen our faith, commitment, and communion of life with him.

I did not say "Saint" Padre Pio for a reason. At that moment in time Pope John Paul II had not yet canonized him. The Devotion to the most Holy Face of Jesus was growing rapidly, and so many miracles were happening throughout the world!

3.05 Jail Bird

One day, one of my friends wanted to make a pilgrimage to Fatima on the Feast of Our Lady of Fatima. We had already paid for the trip, when two detectives came to tell me that I was needed as a witness in a court case.

I explained that I would accept, as long as it was not between the 10th and 18th of May. If I did not go to Fatima, the other person would not go and he would lose his deposit, which he could not afford.

On the day we were leaving, however, I received a call saying that I must be in court on May 13. It was not an important case. I would not let my friend down, so I called my office to say good-bye and was told that the police would be waiting for me at the airport.

It may have been foolish, but we drove to New York where our plane was leaving for Fatima. In the end, it was an exceptional trip, especially for my friend. He was a shy person, yet was asked to carry a flag in honor of our Blessed Mother. We received many graces and blessings on this pilgrimage.

When we returned to Montreal, the next day two detectives showed up at my office and brought me to jail. Of course, I was not too surprised. When they brought me to jail, the guard did all he could to insult me; and, of course, called me "a religious fanatic". I have been called this often. You see, they can't say, "Oh, he loves Jesus with all his heart, his soul, his mind and his body, and we do not love Jesus".

They call us fanatics so that they would not look bad. *"Blessed are those who are persecuted for righteousness' sake, for theirs is the kingdom of Heaven.*

Blessed are you when men revile you and persecute you and utter all kinds of evil against you falsely on my account. Rejoice and be glad for your reward is great in heaven, for so men persecuted the prophets who were before you" (Matthew 5:10-12).

Before going to bed, all the prisoners were brought into a room for a small break. To my amazement, a large group gathered around me and I started to talk to them about the Holy Face of Jesus. We all knelt down to pray. One of the young men said to me, "What am I doing here? I want to become a priest"!

All of them took whatever medals I had. The next morning, they attached chains to my arms and legs and brought me to court. I united myself with St. Paul, the apostle who had been familiar with prison and courts of law. I felt so peaceful. In court I noticed one of the detectives there looking at me in a very strange manner. It was as if all present considered me part of a conspiracy. No matter what they did, they could not disturb my peace, which I sensed they saw in me but could not understand.

Then the judge said to the lawyer, "Do with him what you want"! I looked back at the judge with pity, thinking, "Poor man, in what state will you be when you stand before your God"? I was brought back in chains to my cell.

That night, I asked my Blessed Mother, if it were possible for me to be let out, for I believed that I had done what I had been sent to do and my mother was very worried about me. At approximately ten o'clock that evening, my friend came and got me out of jail - thank God!

3.06 Love's Plea

Without the grace of our Heavenly Father, no one can go to the Son of God. *"No one can come to me unless the Father who sent me draws him"* (John 6.44). We are helpless without the grace of the Son of God. *"I am the way, I am the truth, and I am the life; no one comes to the Father but by me"* (John 14:6).

The source of all knowledge and life is God, our Father. Without the Father, it is impossible to know the Son, and to go to him, the **Incarnate Word**. This is why Jesus declares, *"No one can come to me unless they are drawn by the Father who sent me"* (John 6:44).

Our Heavenly father is calling His children to come and gaze upon the Face of His beloved Son. *"You did not choose Me, I chose you"* (John 15.16).

"By means of my Holy Face the salvation of many souls will be obtained" (Our Lord to Mother Pierina 1936). "Offer my Holy Face without ceasing to the Eternal Father with this offering; you will obtain the salvation and sanctification of many souls" (Our Lord to Mother Pierina 1938).

Who is it that refuses to hear this plea? *"Whoever gazes upon me already consoles me"*. Our Lord seems to be pleading to be loved!

"If my people who are called by my name humble themselves, and pray and seek my Face, and turn from their wicked ways, then I will hear from heaven and will forgive their sin and will heal their land" (2 Chronicles 7.14).

The treasure of the Holy Face in itself possesses such tremendous value, that through it, all the affairs of the church and world can readily be settled. This is not just "a devotion"; this is a divine work of love and mercy that you meditate until the day you die; at which time, it becomes a transport of love, where you behold God, face-to-face forever in eternity.

3.07 **The Book**

The more people wrote about the Holy Face, the more. I realized that we needed to put a book together, which would explain the devotion, and provide a few instructions. So after approximately six months, we put out a book called *The Treasure of the Holy Face of Jesus*. This book contains "the Holy Face Holy Hour"; as well as explanations of the reasons for this devotion; what the popes say about the devotion, the Litany of the Holy Face, and a special novena.

I was inspired to spread a special Novena to the Holy Face of Jesus. This novena was to be brought forth by prayer, on my knees, over a ten-day period. Each day of the novena corresponded to one day's prayer.

The tenth day was to celebrate "The Feast of the Holy Face" by a special consecration of oneself to the Holy Face of Jesus. It was to be called, "The Alpha Omega Holy Face Novena".

Chapter 4 – **Reapers of Grace**

4.01 **Suicide to Priest**

One day, we received a letter from a young man in Africa who was asking for a Holy Face medal. I had a feeling that I should enclose the *Treasure of the Holy Face* book. About one month later, we received a letter from that same man:

"Because I wanted to change my religion and become a Catholic, my parents put me out of the house, and they no longer wanted to see me.

In Africa, families are very close and I truly felt very bad, so much so, that I had made up my mind to commit suicide. I knew exactly how it would be done, I had bought all that I needed to do it. The day was picked, as well as the hour.

That same day, your parcel arrived. I put the Holy Face medal around my neck and read the book, *The Treasure of the Holy Face of Jesus.* Not only did I not commit suicide - but also, after reading the book, I made up my mind to become a priest. Thanks be to God!" (P.M., Africa. Note: As of this writing, this young man is in the priesthood.)

4.02 **Understand the Devotion**

I will now try to explain this devotion to the most Holy Face of Jesus. Pope Pius IX said, "This salutary reparation to the Holy Face of Jesus is a Divine work, destined to save modern society".

I could quote many other popes on this devotion, but Pope Pius IX tells the true meaning: Our Lord has not left us orphans (John 14:18). As a loving Father, he has sent us "divine means" to overcome all the evils of these days, but we must remember that we still have our "free will" by which we accept or reject these God-given gifts.

St. Francis was weeping bitter tears at the foot of the cross. His brother asked him: "Why are you weeping"? St. Francis replied: "Because he has suffered so much for so many, and they are so forgetful of him".

Many saints had a devotion to the Holy Face of Jesus (It would be too long to mention them all). A few include: St. Augustine, St. Bernard, St. Gertrude the Great and St. Mechtilde (her sister), St. Padre Pio (of course), St. Thérèse of the Child Jesus, and the Holy Face, etc. The list goes on.

St. Augustine said, "Love is not loved"! But does one not always seek the face of the one they love? What is true love? The Holy Bible says,

"Lord, show us your Face and we shall be healed" (Psalm 80:3).

"Seek the Lord and his strength, seek his presence continually" (Psalm 104:4).

"Such is the generation of those who seek the face of the God of Jacob" (Psalm 24:6).

To refuse the Holy Face of Jesus is to refuse the love and the cross that brought about our redemption.

Let us go back to the time before the crucifixion, to the birth of Jesus. Jesus is born of the Virgin Mary. Jesus is the Son of God, sent to redeem the whole of mankind. So, Mary is the Mother of Jesus and in very plain words, Mary is the Mother of God.

At the wedding feast of Cana, when Jesus was thirty years old, our Blessed Mother asked him to work his first miracle by changing the water into wine. But, I believe that at the same time, she gave her consent for Jesus to start the work of the redemption of souls.

At the crucifixion, our Lord said, *"Woman, behold thy son"*, and to his disciple John, *"behold thy Mother"* (John 19:26-27). At that time, Jesus established a new spiritual relationship. We all became children of Mary, the Mother of God. She accepted us all as her children.

Jesus gave all his sufferings and his life that we may be redeemed, and he knew how the evil one would do all in his power to make us his slaves; slaves to our passions, slaves to money, slaves to power, and slaves of evil desires of every kind.

How simple it is today to fall into grievous sins; sins of the second death. A mortal sin is "a sin of the second death".

We are children of Mary. Imagine how truly loved we are! We are children of the Mother of God!

We are heirs of Christ! We have been adopted as sons and daughters of God! This is what God is: absolute love, perfect love.

When we are born again, in plain words, when we are baptized, we become heirs, children of God.

How can we return this love? How can we share in this kind of love? This is why I have to tell this story. It is the story of a sinner, because that is what I am. But through the grace of God, through our Blessed Mother, St. Joseph, and all the saints; the angels and all the heavenly hosts who we belong to, and who are striving daily to help us on the narrow road to Heaven – wonders are performed.

Our Blessed Mother Mary is truly a mother. And what does a good mother do? She watches over her children. Is that not natural? What kind of mother would not care about what her children are doing? A mother makes sure there is no danger when her children are playing, and when they cry they receive a hug and a cheerful word.

The children have confidence in their mother, and can totally rely on her being there, no matter what. When they hurt themselves, or are sick, she is there to help them get better, no matter how young or how old the child is. In the eyes of the mother, they are always her children, and she is always their mother.

How much more is the Blessed Mother to all her children? She has come to us in so many different places to show us what we should do to get to

Heaven. Our Blessed Mother is already in heaven, but she is attentive to her children, which is why our Mother appeared so often: at La Salette, Lourdes, Fatima, etc. She also appeared to special, chosen souls, like St. Catherine Labouré (whose body is incorrupt) with the message of "The Miraculous Medal" and all its promises. Over the years, she has come to different saints with special messages.

Our Blessed Mother came with Jesus to Sister Saint Pierre (born in 1816), and gave many messages about the importance of making reparation to the most Holy Face of Jesus. Sister Saint Pierre was told of the most terrible sin of "blasphemy" that even children were committing. A special prayer was given to her, called the "Golden Arrow", which would pierce his heart and make reparation for this worst of sins.

Our Lord told Sister Saint-Pierre, "Rejoice my daughter, because the hour approaches when the most beautiful work under the sun will be born." Sister Saint-Pierre died in 1848 in the "odor of sanctity". Twenty-five years after she died, St. Thérèse of the Child Jesus and the Holy Face was born in 1873.

St. Thérèse told her novices that the Holy Face was the book from which she learned "the science of love" and "the art of practicing all the virtues".

St. Thérèse also said that devotion to the Holy Face was "the crown of her love for the Sacred Humanity of our Lord". It was from the contemplation of the Holy Face of Jesus that St.

Thérèse drew her strength for all her courageous acts of virtue. It was in the meditation of the humiliated Face of Jesus that she learned detachment from creatures to love, suffering, and self-sacrifice.

St. Thérèse said, "I would gladly live 1000 lives, if it would save one soul". So, who can begin to try and explain the value of one soul in the eyes of God?

St. Thérèse on devotion to the Holy Face: "When you love someone, you look at his face, not at his heels or his shoulders. Souls are being lost like flakes of snow, Celine, let us be apostles."

At the Canonization of St. Thérèse, Mother Agnes, the superior, said that St. Thérèse had a gentle devotion to "the Infant Jesus", but it did not compare with that which she had for "The Holy Face of Jesus". St. Thérèse died in 1897.

4.03 Comes to Light

Our Heavenly Father had prepared the world for this moment. Less than one year after the death of St. Thérèse, the whole world was shaken by a "Great Mystery". In 1898, a photographer had taken a picture of the Holy Shroud, and it revealed the image of a majestic crucified man - the actual image of Jesus Christ, Son of the Living God!

For the first time in the history of humanity, the actual image of 'the most holy face of Jesus crucified' was shown to the whole world. It had been hidden for 1898 years. It had been hidden and revealed to our generation, a generation in which there is a great lack of faith. It had been reserved for this age, the age of television; the age of the computer; and the age when one must 'see to believe'.

The most beautiful work under the sun had been born, the most simple and natural devotion in the whole world. We do not hide the face of the loved-one, the one we seek!

However, mankind still did not accept this tremendous gift from our Heavenly Father; they were still doubtful. Many did not believe.

"Whoever does not receive the Kingdom of God like a child shall not enter it" (Mark 10:15).

Mother Pierina's spiritual director said that one day, the pope would tell the whole world of the importance of the Holy Face devotion and the Holy Face medal.

It is an easy means of obtaining the salvation of sinners and our own salvation; a powerful means to bring peace to the soul, peace to the world, and to bring back to Christ many who have abandoned him. But wait, just what does this mean? Why did this happen? What is our Heavenly Father trying to show his children?

Remember, "holy simplicity". Let us take this slowly! There are many books written about the Holy Shroud, some for, and some against. Many would like you to just forget the whole thing as if it never happened. First, always seek the advice of a wise man. Pope Pius XI gave pictures of the Holy Face from the Holy Shroud to youths saying, "They are pictures of the Divine Son of Mary; they come, in fact, from that object known as the Shroud of Turin, still mysterious, but certainly not the work of any human hand".

This is what I cannot get over: how many thousands of people came from all over the world, traveling thousands of miles to gaze upon the Holy Shroud. They did this for hundreds of years, never realizing the secret contained by the Holy Shroud, which had been reserved for our days (until modern photography would reveal it) - the days of television and computers; the age when many people from all over the world would lose the faith (Pope John Paul II stated that the reason there are so many problems in the world today is due to a great lack of faith).

How is this so? The Holy Shroud's actual positive image is what is called a "natural negative". Who could possibly leave a negative image, which would turn positive only when the camera was invented, when one would take a picture of it then and only then would we see the positive image, the actual Holy Face of Jesus, our Lord and our God?

What had been hidden for 1898 years is now revealed to the whole world. The whole body of the Crucified Jesus, front and back, with all its sufferings, is there for all to see. Like St. Thomas, we are now in a position to see with our own eyes, and can respond with, "*My Lord and my God*" (John 20:28-29). Who could possibly refuse to believe, except those who choose not to believe! We live in an age where one must see in order to believe.

4.04 **The Remedy**

So many today ask, "How much longer will our Heavenly Father put up with all that is happening in the world today? When will God do something to change the world? When will he hear our pleas for help?"

God has sent us a most powerful means to change the whole world! The most Holy Face of his beloved son Jesus, with whom he is well pleased!

Because we are little children, our Heavenly Father teaches us in stages. One of the major problems today, is that people are trying to make everything so difficult. Do you not remember what Jesus said: "*Truly, I say to you, unless you turn and become like children, you will never enter the kingdom of heaven.*" (Matthew 18:3).

How about what Saint Francis said: "Oh, holy simplicity". He was so impressed with simplicity, that he called it holy! We can often become our own worst enemy. And we must learn when we have gone to confession that we must also forgive ourselves and turn completely to Jesus in total surrender and trust, having confidence in his tremendous love.

We are all called to be apostles. The Holy Spirit pushes us, and keeps on pushing. He works in us, invites us, and even though we are free, he pushes us to follow his inspiration. And who will remember us 100, 500 or 1,000 years from now? We pass this way but once, for a very short period of time. And, what we amass spiritually is all that we bring with us for the whole of eternity.

So many souls are crying to be helped; we have a God-given destiny to help our brothers and sisters to find the truth – JESUS.

This great devotion to the Holy Face of Jesus Christ, given to us by our Heavenly Father, is a powerful remedy (antidote) for these days of such great temptations and tests of faith. By helping others to know of this awesome gift of our Heavenly Father, we also receive many graces and blessings for our own perseverance.

In helping others to love and console Jesus and to make daily reparation, we are performing the *"works of faith"* by our good deeds (James 2:20). Many fail to appreciate the greatness of this gift. Lord, increase our faith (Luke 17:5)!

4.05 Holy Hour

The "Holy Face Holy Hour of Reparation" was started with the help of a wonderful priest named Father David. We would get between 15 to 30 people who came to this Holy Hour.

One day I asked Jesus, "Why don't you work a miracle so that we can get a lot more people to come to the Holy Hour?"

Our Lord answered, *"Yes I could work a miracle and then the church would be full and many would be in the street waiting to enter the church, but then they would be coming for themselves. Those who come now, do so because of me*". I answered, "Please, Jesus don't work a miracle. I would much rather have quality then quantity".

Another day, during the Holy Face Holy Hour of Reparation on Sunday between 3:00 p.m., and 4:00 p.m., at the Franciscan Church, we had approximately fifteen people. During the Holy Hour, Our Lord inspired me to thank everyone for being there; that they were making reparation for all those who do not go to church on Sundays, who treat him like a mock king (by treating him like a fool). How very sad! "Blasphemy" and the "desecration of Sunday" are the two principal sins in modern time.

The attacks upon Holy Mother Church (the Bride of Christ) and the lack of respect for the Eucharist are a renewal of the blows received by his Sacred Face during the passion. These are a renewal of how they laughed at him, slapped him, spit upon him, and mocked him by calling him names. At that time, only a few executioners crucified him on Good Friday – but today countless numbers of Christians crucify him every Sunday.

4.06 **A Revelation**

One day, I went to see a movie (I don't remember the name of it) but the theatre was full of people. As I watched the movie, it started to show something that violated purity. I closed my eyes and said, "Jesus and Mary, keep me pure of heart, soul, mind and body, so that I may see God". All of a sudden, when I reopened my eyes, the movie screen disappeared. I could see the actors, actresses, and directors appear in front of me. The screen was no longer there. Instead, all the actors, actresses, directors, etc., appeared alive, in front of me, on the stage.

I questioned why this was happening and why it was shown to me. The understanding I received was that when we are shown evil, be it at the movies, on television, or on the Internet, etc., we become participants in the evil that is proposed for our entertainment, because we agree with it by the assent of our own intellect and will.

4.07 **Blessed Signs**

Our Lord is asking, "Who desires to love me?" Our Lady of La Salette warned us to obey the commandments of God, and to keep Sunday holy. Go to church on Sunday. Make reparation for the tremendous sins of blasphemy and for the profanation of Sunday. Modern man has lost the concept of prayer. Jesus, surely, is very sad at the state in which the world is today. I do not have to go into detail. We have been given so many warnings through our Blessed Mother. Jesus wishes us to make reparation for the sins of the world.

Our Blessed Mother is intensely concerned with our salvation. She wishes, through Mother Pierina, to tell the whole world about the graces, which anyone can obtain by offering the divine face of Jesus to our Heavenly Father. No drop of Jesus' blood should be shed in vain. It was shed for our eternal happiness; and, we must keep in mind and look towards our true home with God in heaven.

The devotion to the Holy Face of Jesus is needed in our world. It is here to renew the Church. The soul is the battlefield between God and Satan. The shield of protection is the Holy Face of Jesus. If you wish to receive the promises... wear the Holy Face and Blessed Sacrament medal (with faith) as proof of your belonging to God – so that you may receive the special protection and blessings as promised by our Blessed Mother.

It is very important to remember our Blessed Mother first came to Mother Maria Pierina with the "Holy Face Cloth Scapular". The medal of the Holy Face was substituted with the same promises and may be used instead of the cloth scapular. Therefore, it is to be worn around your neck, as your sign of "total consecration to Jesus" until the day you die.

On one side is the image of the Holy Face of Jesus. On the other side is an image of the Blessed Sacrament (the Eucharistic Host). By the wearing of this blessed medal you are confirming not only that you consecrate your life to Jesus, but also that you believe He is truly present in the Holy Eucharist: Body, Blood, Soul and Divinity. *"The bread, which I shall give for the life of the world is my flesh"* (John 6:51).

"He who eats my flesh and drinks my blood abides in me, and I in him" (John 6:56). Who would be so foolish as to refuse this gift? I beg you, "Please help your brothers and sisters to know about this treasure". Very truly, it is your responsibility to do so!

4.08 **John Paul II**

Pope John Paul II warned Christians to be ready to give their lives for their faith, the supreme testimony of blood for the sake of truth and justice, in the presence of modern day Herods. All Christians must be ready to give constant witness each day - even at the cost of suffering and serious sacrifice. We cannot compromise.

One day our spiritual director was going to see Pope John Paul II. I was preparing a truly beautiful Holy Face picture on wood, which an artist had donated to the Association. I said why don't you offer this picture to Pope John Paul II? When the priest returned from his meeting with the Pope, I asked him what had happened? He said that when he gave the Pope the Holy Face picture (from the Holy Shroud), the Pope said to him, "Do you know what you have given me"? The priest said he did not answer. Then Pope John Paul II continued, "You have just given me the actual image of Jesus Christ, Son of God". And when the priests who were helping the Pope came to put away all the gifts he had received, which included the Holy Face picture, Pope John Paul said, "No!" and he put his two arms around the Holy Face picture and went off to his room. How pleased I was he had chosen our gift to place in his private chamber.

4.09 **The Apostolate**

Love knows no bounds. As St. Francis said, "Let us start, for up to now we have done nothing". This is the opportunity we have been given to help save precious souls. Let us not waste time (time is short); let us "put out into the deep..." as Pope John Paul II said just before his death.

St. Paul speaks of the superior wisdom of faith, *"For I decided to know nothing among you except Jesus Christ and him crucified"* (1 Corinthians 2:2). Devotion to the Holy Face of Jesus is a matter of faith. And faith calls us to action.

4.10 **The Vigil**

My mother who helped to spread this devotion with my daughter and me were with us at The Easter Vigil. She was not well. During the Mass I heard her sigh and looked at her and said, "What is wrong"? She said, "When the priest lifted up the Chalice, I saw a white light coming out of the Chalice. It came very slowly and gently. My mouth was open just a little and it came into my mouth and through my body". She had received a gift from the Holy Spirit. How pleased I was for her.

My mother told me how these were the best days of her life, and how she enjoyed doing our Lord's work. When she received the "Sacrament of Anointing of the Sick", she had the appearance of a little child with spring flowers in her hair. She had become like that little child Jesus spoke about (Matthew 18:3). In a very short period of time, she went to her reward. I know she is waiting for me to share in her happiness. Thank you Lord for the gift of my mother! Thank you for her sacrifice and dedication. Thank you for her simplicity and her great love. Thank you!

Chapter 5 – **Resurrecting The Shroud**

5.01 **The Shroud**

The picture on the following page shows how Jesus was wrapped in a burial cloth, and how his body was covered front and back (figure 1, page 60).

The Shroud provides evidence that he was tortured and beaten.

It also reveals the nail wounds on the wrists and on the feet, as well as a wound on the right side of the chest, where a spear pierced the heart.

In addition, the Shroud reveals the terrible scourging on the front and the back of the body, and the blood, which flowed from the wounds.

The Shroud is a sepia color (yellowish, brown). The height of Jesus is 1.80 meters tall, and shows long hair, a beard, and a moustache. The beard is called a "forked bead".

The Shroud's dimensions are 4.37 meters long and 1.11 meters wide.

Figure 1

In figure 2, on page 64, you will see two different views of the Holy Shroud. It shows how the Holy Shroud looks to the naked eye.

Thousands of people, who did not realize it was meant for our generation, venerated it because, in our day, many must see to believe.

The Holy Shroud is a perfect negative, an opposite of a positive. This miracle was waiting for the camera to be invented.

One day, a lawyer named Secondo Pia took photographs of the Holy Shroud, and to the amazement of all, a positive image of the Holy Shroud was shown for the first time (see figure 3, page 73).

For the first time in 1,898 years, the whole world was able to see the actual image of Jesus, Son of the living God!

Our Heavenly Father knew that our generation would need to see the image of his beloved son, Jesus.

As our Lord told Sister St. Pierre, "*Soon the most beautiful work under the Sun will be born*".

In figures 2 and 3, page 64, you see the full view of the Holy Shroud: negative and positive images (the whole body, front and back).

To my knowledge, many have tried to explain how this image was formed, but none have been able to do so, nor can they reproduce another shroud with all their knowledge!

The Holy Shroud is the only cloth in the whole world to have a three dimensional image. On the eyes, as you will see, are two coins, minted in the seven year reign of Pontius Pilate (see figure 10), which by itself places the Holy Shroud to the time of the Crucifixion

We must remember that what we are seeing through the Grace of God is the actual image of His Beloved Son, Jesus; and the record of all His suffering: the punches he received; the slaps in the face; the spittle from vile mouths; and the crown of thorns.

He was made fun of and treated like a joke. Has anything changed? How many today treat Jesus with disrespect! We are permitted to see the awful scourging that He endured, so that we might be saved, and yet people refuse to believe. How sad!

Look at the image of Jesus (figure 5, page 66)! Gaze upon him! You see his naked image, and yet, you sense "His Majesty", which evokes the highest respect.

The majestic humility of his countenance amidst profound suffering is a witness to who He is: Jesus Christ, "King of Heaven and of Earth". Shame on those who refuse to believe!

Some say, "What about the Carbon 14 dating"? Well, what about it? Common sense tells you they made a mistake!

They took a cloth sample from an area in the corner that had been repaired (a piece of cloth was added) before a fire in 1532. This also included part of a seam, which had also been added during the Middle Ages to support the backing. Carbon deposits therefore, contaminated this corner, which was affected by the fire of 1532.

The corners of the Shroud are the most contaminated because many hands held them, leaving human sweat and oil, and whatever else was on their hands. The contaminations happened over many centuries.

I quote Dr. Robert Oppenheimer, the father of the atomic bomb, who said: "There are many doors science can open, but there is still one door that can be opened only by God".

On September 5, 1995, in an address on Italian television, the archbishop of Turin at that time, Cardinal Giovanni Saldarini, stated: "The image on the Shroud is that of Christ, and no one else!"

The Cardinal made it clear that he did not speak for himself, but for the Shroud's legal owner at that time, Pope John Paul II; and for the Vatican, who had entrusted him, as the cloth's custodian, with conveying their intentions.

In order to see things more clearly, we will look at more details in some of the images on the following pages.

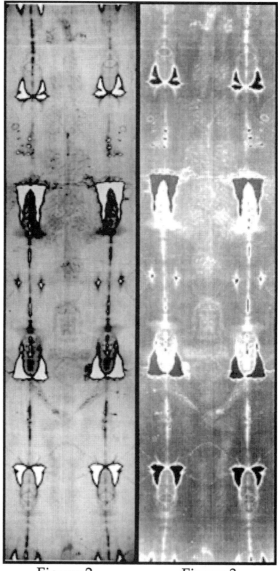

Figure 2   Figure 3

In figure 4, without any visual aids to the naked eye, we see the "photographic positive" (the film when developed and printed) frontal image of Jesus, which appears to be the "photographic negative" (the film after a picture is taken but before it is developed).

On each side of the Holy Shroud are two lines of scorch marks covered by triangular patches.

The Holy Shroud was in a fire during the night between the third and fourth of December in 1532, in the Sainte Chapelle in Chambery.

A drop of molten metal from the casket, which contained the Shroud, penetrated the Shroud cloth and caused a pattern of damage because the Shroud was folded into 48 layers.

The water used to put out the fire also left watermarks on the Shroud.

The Poor Clares (Franciscan nuns) had put patches on the Shroud because they wanted to preserve and protect it when it was being shown in public.

Pope John Paul II described the Holy Shroud as the "Icon of the Passion".

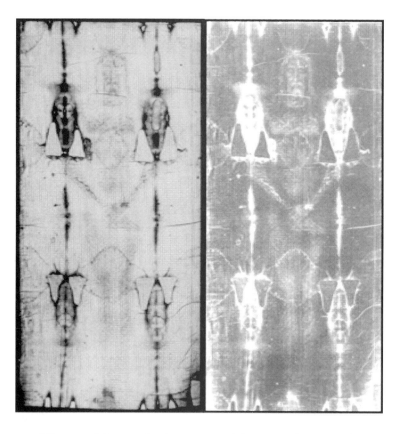

Figure 4 (negative)   **Figure 5** (positive)

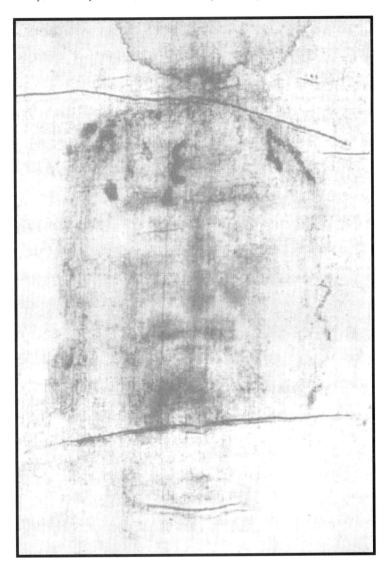

Figure 6 (negative)

Please notice the appearance of the face in figure 6. The "positive" image actually appears to the naked eye as a "negative"!

This is not natural because the Holy Shroud image is, to all appearances, a negative. This is the image that people have seen yet has eluded them for 1,898 years!

Now, in figure 7, let us look at the actual image of Jesus from the Holy Shroud after the advent of modern photography. As mentioned earlier, many have tried to reproduce the image on the Holy Shroud but, of course, have not succeeded. The image on the Shroud is three dimensional, and there is only one such cloth in the world.

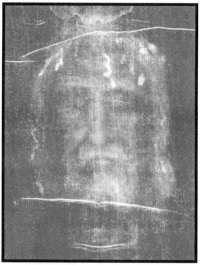

Figure 7 (positive)

At long last, the actual image of Jesus, our Lord and our God! Now, on the Holy Face of Jesus, you can actually see the love, as well as the suffering he endured for each of us.

The white drops you see on the Holy Face of Jesus are blood. One also sees majestic patience, humility, and total self-giving.

This is the tremendous gift our Heavenly Father gave us. His message shines forth from the light we see on the most Holy Face of Jesus (Matthew 4:16). This light is the way to overcome every problem in today's world.

One cannot look at the Holy Face of Jesus without seeing what our sins have done. We must imitate our Lord's model of silence and complete surrender. It is the example of how to grow in Divine Love, which Jesus referred to when he said, *"No one has greater love than this, to lay down one's life for one's friends"* (John 15:13).

Please remember that he also said, *"And whoever sees me sees him who sent me"* (John 12:45). St. Paul says, "The light of the glory of God on the face of Jesus Christ" (2 Cor. 4:6).

Holy Face Medal
(front and back view)

Figure 8

Venerable Servant of God

Mother Maria Pierina de Micheli

Of the daughters of the Immaculate Conception of

Buenos Aires (1890 -1945)

5.02 **Mother Pierina**

Let us return to the story of Mother Pierina. While she was confiding to Jesus one of her trials, he appeared to her, bleeding and with an expression of sorrow and tenderness, "that I will never forget", she writes. Jesus said to her, "*What have I done*"? Mother Pierina understood immediately, and the Holy Face of Jesus became her book of meditation.

On the First Friday of Lent in 1936, Jesus, with his face covered with blood, and with profound sadness, said to her, "*I wish that my face which reflects the intimate pains of my soul, the suffering, and the love of my heart, be more honored. He who meditates upon me consoles me*".

On the Tuesday of Passion Week, our Lord returned to Mother Pierina and said, "*Every time that my face is contemplated, I will pour my love into the hearts of men, and through my holy face, will be obtained the salvation of many souls*". Our Lord also told her that, "*It is possible that some souls are fearful, that the devotion of my holy face will decrease the devotion to my sacred heart. Tell them that on the contrary, it shall be completed and increased. Contemplating my face, souls shall participate in my sufferings. They will feel the necessity to love and make reparation. Isn't this perhaps the true devotion to my sacred heart*"?

After this explanation, the devotion to the Holy Face did not permit any doubt. Christian piety has always found in this bloodstained face a new road to reparation and to love, and certainly all devotees of the Sacred Heart will also reflect upon the Holy Face, which is the joy of the angels and of the saints. The devotees of the Sacred Heart will, therefore, find in the Holy Face, the perfection of devotion. In the Holy Face, they will find the external expression of the Sacred Heart's love for human beings. These manifestations from Jesus were made always more pressing, and in March of 1938, while she was praying, a beautiful Lady appeared to her near the altar in a stream of light. She held in her hands a scapular formed of two pieces of white flannel, united by a cord. One piece bore the Image of the Holy Face of Jesus, around which was inscribed "*Illumina Domine Vultum Tuum Super Nos*" – "May, O Lord, the light of Thy countenance shine upon us" (Psalm 67:1). On the reverse was a Host surrounded by rays with the inscription "*Mane Nobiscum, Domine*" – "Stay with us, O Lord" (Luke 24:29).

The Lady approached her slowly and said:

"Listen well, and refer all that I say to the Father. This scapular is a weapon of defense, a shield of courage, a guarantee of love and of mercy that Jesus wishes to give to the world in these times of sexuality and of hatred towards God and his Church. Diabolical snares are laid to steer the faith from the hearts of men, evil is spreading, true apostles are few, a divine remedy is necessary, and this remedy is the Holy Face of Jesus! All those who shall wear a scapular such as this, and make, if they can, a visit to the Blessed Sacrament every Tuesday in reparation for the outrages received by the Holy Face of my Son Jesus, during his passion, and those which He receives daily in the Sacrament of the Eucharist, will be fortified in the faith, ready to defend it, and to overcome all difficulties interior and exterior. Furthermore, they will have a happy death under the loving gaze of my Divine Son".

For participation in the wonderful benefits of this devotion, Jesus did not require much. A visit to the Blessed Sacrament each Tuesday is really not a difficult thing, while the benefits that will come to our souls will be immense! How beautiful to know that a look of compassion from that Face, disfigured by our sins, will merit for us the privilege of contemplating it eternally in the splendor of his glory.

The command of the Blessed Mother made itself felt even more strongly to Mother Pierina, but it was not in her power to have this command carried out.

In the same year, Jesus appeared to her again, still dripping with blood and with great sadness, said:

"See how much I suffer? And still I am little understood. What ingratitude on the part of those who claim to love me! I have given my heart as the sensible object of my great love for men, and I give my face as the sensible object of my sufferings for the sins of men. I wish that it be honored with a particular feast on the Tuesday of Quinquagesima, (Shrove Tuesday - the Tuesday just before Ash Wednesday). The feast is to be preceded by a novena, in which all the faithful shall make reparation with me, uniting themselves to the participation of my sufferings".

In 1940, Mother Pierina obtained permission to have a medal struck. The first one was presented to our Holy Father, Pope Pius XII. The work of distributing it began and soon it became associated with the miraculous. Soldiers, civilians, men, women, the young and the old, the sick and the well, the imprisoned, persons in concentration camps, Christians, Jews - all felt God's prodigious power. On earth, on the sea, in airplanes, submarines, an infinite number of graces and miracles have been obtained.

Enraged by this, the devil attacked Mother Pierina to frighten her and impede the distribution of the medal. He flung the medals through the corridors and down the stairs and tore down the images and pictures of the Holy Face; but she endured everything. She suffered and offered it up so that the Holy Face would be honored.

Mother Maria Pierina was somewhat perturbed because she had medals made instead of scapulars, and so she turned to the Blessed Mother for reassurance.

On April 7, 1943 the Blessed Virgin appeared to her and said, "My daughter, be tranquil. Be tranquil because the medal, with the same promises and favors, substitutes for the scapular. It only needs to be more diffused. Now, dear to my heart, is the Feast of the Holy Face of My Divine Son. Tell the Pope that I am much concerned".

Our Lady was complaining about how little devotion people had to the Holy Face of our Lord, and said that it was this particular Devotion that will help people overcome their difficulties. This Devotion would also act as a special defense for mankind.
– (revelation of the Blessed Mother to Maria Pierina)

5.03 **The Five Promises**

1. Grace to keep the faith
2. Courage to confess the faith
3. Special help in external difficulties
4. Special help in difficulties of the soul
5. Grace to die a happy death

How happy shall be our death if we die gazing on the Face of our dear Lord!

Who is it that refuses to hear this plea? *"Whoever gazes upon me already consoles me"*. Surely, it is urgent and necessary for us to help souls to know of this devotion, a providential remedy for these days. *"If my people, who are called by my name, shall humble themselves, and pray and seek my face, and turn from their wicked ways, then I will hear from heaven, and will forgive their sins, and will heal their land"* (2 Chronicles 7:14).

Jesus said to Mother Pierina, *"...with this offering you will obtain the salvation and sanctification of many souls; when, however, you will offer it through my priests, miracles will be worked"*.

Another time he said, *"Now, if there will still be those who will not recognize that this is truly my work, it is because they close their eyes"*.

5.04 **Deeper Meanings**

The Holy Face message can be compared to the message of Naaman, in the Book of Kings, when Naaman presented a letter to the King of Israel:

"When this letter reaches you, know that I have sent to you my servant Naaman, that you may cure him of his leprosy." When the king of Israel read the letter, he tore his clothes and said, "Am I God, to give death or life, that this man sends word to me to cure a man of his leprosy? Just look and see how he is trying to pick a quarrel with me." But when Elisha the man of God heard that the king of Israel had torn his clothes, he sent a message to the king, "Why have you torn your clothes? Let him come to me, that he may learn that there is a prophet in Israel." So Naaman came with his horses and chariots, and halted at the entrance of Elisha's house. Elisha sent a messenger to him, saying, "Go, wash in the Jordan seven times, and your flesh shall be restored and you shall be clean." But Naaman became angry and went away, saying, "I thought that for me he would surely come out, and stand and call on the name of the Lord his God, and would wave his hand over the spot, and cure the leprosy! Are not Abana and Pharpar, the rivers of Damascus, better than all the waters of Israel? Could I not wash in them, and be clean?" He turned and went away in a rage. But his servants approached and said to him, "Father, if the prophet had commanded you to do something difficult, would you not have done it? How much more, when all he said to you was, "Wash, and be clean"? So he went down and immersed himself seven times in the Jordan, according to the word of the man of God; his flesh was restored like the flesh of a young boy, and he was clean" (2 Kings 5:7-14).

How can our Heavenly Father make it any simpler for his children to come to his Beloved Son, Jesus? By wearing the Holy Face medal around your neck, you consecrate your life totally to Jesus. Ask Jesus to take over your life. You will be wearing a very powerful sacramental, and usually in a very short period of time, you will receive the grace to grow rapidly in the love of God. Or, you can refuse to do so. If Naaman had gone home, he would never have been cured of his leprosy. And, our sin is much worse than leprosy.

By wearing the Holy Face Blessed Sacrament medal, we become warriors of the most Holy Face of Jesus, fighting on the "Battlefield of Faith". Our Lord places his two arms around our necks, and goes in front of us with his love and protection in loving concern for His children.

God sees all that we do. The angels watch, always at our side. What honor, glory, and joy it is to do battle in the presence of God!

Our warfare is not waged with the weapons of this world. We arm ourselves with the shield of faith and with the sword of the spirit, which is the word of God (2 Cor. 10:3-4; Eph. 6: 16-17).

We must prepare ourselves for the ultimate struggle between good over evil. It is only through the humanity of Jesus that we will be sanctified and that we will be saved. It is essential that we live in close friendship with Jesus and with our blessed, caring Mother. We must cling to them so as not to be carried away by the torrents of evil that threaten us.

Now, to prove to you that this devotion comes from our Heavenly Father for our days, let us look on the most Holy Face of Jesus, which was hidden for 1,898 years. Remember that our Blessed Mother said this is a powerful antidote to overcome all the evils of these days; and one certainly cannot overcome them without faith, and fortitude, and God's grace.

On the Holy Face of Jesus, is a perfect "Ex 3", which the scriptural citation for the book of Exodus chapter 3, verse 14 (figure 11), where our Lord says to Moses, *"I AM WHO AM"*, in very plain words for all to read. Our Lord is saying, *"I AM GOD"*! This was not seen on the Holy Face shroud before the miracle photograph, because it was not yet meant to be.

You can also see the number "3" on the forehead for the Trinity, meaning three persons in one God. There is also a perfect cross that can be seen. With Jesus, we will always see the "cross".

Now, on one side of the medal is the Holy Face of Jesus, and on the other is the Blessed Sacrament. When we turn the picture of the most Holy Face of Jesus upside down, we will see a chalice formed with a cross. This is the confirmation we have been given that, in the blood of Christ, poured out for many, we have a remedy to overcome the evils of these days.

When we are offered the Holy Face picture and the Holy Face medal, we still have free choice, to accept the Holy Face of Jesus, and the message, or reject them. The choice is ours but please let me explain what happens to many of those who accept it.

When Jesus walked on the water and told the wind to stop, it did, because he is God. When our Lord walked into a house, the first thing he did was to say "Peace be with you". This was God. When He said, "Peace be with you", the people in that house, who accepted him, felt an actual peace come upon them. This is why they were all following Jesus, not just because he was curing people but also, because they knew he was the way, and the truth - their peace.

When he sent his Apostles into the homes, he would tell them to say, "Peace be with you"! If they do not accept your peace, let it return to you. In other words, our Lord is asking that you give yourself 100% to him – not 99%, but 100%. When you put the Holy Face medal around your neck, it is until the day you die. You are making a total commitment, and are asking Jesus to run your life from now on. You are giving Jesus your total trust and control, in union with our Blessed Mother.

Many people who do this and who truly wish to come close to God, actually feel a tremendous peace come upon them within a short period of time; the same peace that came upon the people when Jesus visited them. Their whole lives can change in a very short period of time and they can grow in the love of Jesus in leaps and bounds, always ready to defend their faith, and help many others to find this fast easy road to heaven.

On the other side of the medal is a picture of the Blessed Sacrament "*Unless you eat the flesh of the Son of man and drink his blood, you have no life in you*" (John 6:53).

"*Those who eat my flesh and drink my blood abide in me, and I in them*" - says the Lord (John 6:56).

Your respect, gratitude, and love for Jesus are reasons why you should attend Sunday Mass and be in the "state of grace".

If you are not in the state of grace please receive the "Sacrament of Reconciliation" in a spirit of sorrow for your sins.

I strongly suggest the importance and the duty of priests to make themselves available in the confessional as did St. Curé d'Ars and St. Padre Pio.

In this way they take the example of our Lord's parable of the Prodigal Son whose father vigilantly awaits his return (Luke 15:20).

In the "Sacrament of Reconciliation", our Lord forgives all your sins through the ministry of the priest.

This is a very fast-paced world where there is much temptation. Therefore, we should be in the habit of going to confession often, to receive both forgiveness and strength to resist the tempter.

How many there are, who receive Jesus unworthily, in a state of serious sin, because there is no priest to hear confession before Mass.

Through his availability in the confessional, the priest witnesses to the importance of being in a state of grace before receiving communion.

Figure 9

Mother Pierina liked this Holy Face portrayal.

Holy Face painting by Bruner

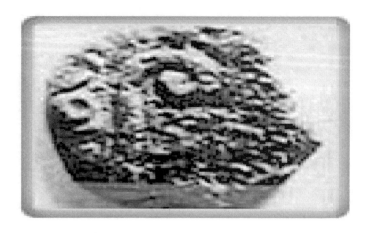

Pilate Lepton

Figure 10
Coin image mage found on Holy Shroud
(*Minted in the 7-year reign of Pontius Pilate*)

On the eyes of the image on the Shroud, there appear two coins. The custom in those days was to keep the eyes closed.

The coins were minted during the seven-year reign of Pontius Pilate. (In figure 10, take note of the image on the coins).

From the crown of thorns on the following page (Figure 11), you will see special blood stains, which symbolically represent and point to the most Holy Trinity - three persons in one God - Father, Son and Holy Spirit.

Explanation of the Burning Bush: (figure 11)

The Ex 3 is a reference to Exodus, chapter 3, where Our Lord says to Moses: "I am who I am" (I am God)

Then Moses said to God:
"If I come to the Israelites and tell them that 'The God of their forefathers has sent me to you', and they ask me his name, what shall I say"? God answered: *"I am who I am"* (Exodus 3:14).

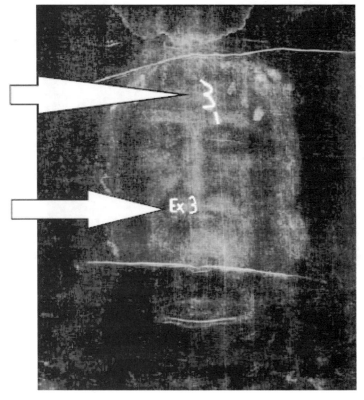

Figure 11
The number 3 symbolizes The Holy Trinity.

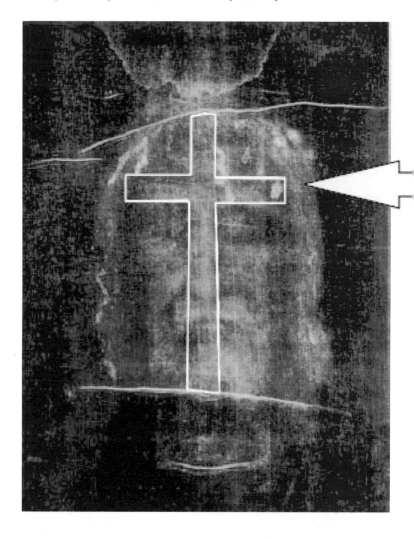

Figure 12 (the Cross)

"I decided to know nothing among you except Jesus Christ, and him crucified" - St. Paul, (1 Corinthians 2:2)

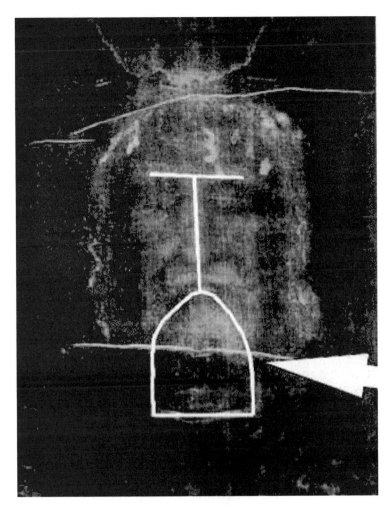

Figure 13 (Chalice)

The upside-down chalice with a perfect cross testifies to the blood of the Lamb poured out to the last drop.

While I am on the subject of the Holy Shroud, talking about Moses, I wish to bring up another matter. In the days of Moses, God asked that the blood of a lamb be put on the doorpost of the homes of his chosen people.

At that time God saved all those who had the sign of the "blood of the Lamb" on their doorposts.

Today, many are not proud of Jesus. I invite them to put on the front door a picture of the Holy Face of Jesus, who is "the Lamb of God" (foretold and pre-figured in the days of Moses).

Remember, Jesus said, "*Those who are ashamed of me and of my words, of them will the Son of man will be ashamed when he comes in his glory and the glory of the Father and of the holy angels*" (Luke 9:26).

We must demonstrate that we belong to the Lord, who purchased our life by his death. We must be unashamed to witness our gratitude. Rest assured that the Lord will be proud of you, and continue to offer you his protection.

Chapter 6 – **Testifying To Love**

6.01 **Bruno's Testimony**

Bruno's story is about a man who wished to place a picture of the Holy Face of Jesus on his front door so he would receive a special protection and so people would see where his true love was.

"For two days I hesitated to put up the door plaque of the Holy Face of Jesus, because I was embarrassed to place a religious object on the front door of my condo where all my neighbors would see it. I was feeling weaker and weaker the more I hesitated, until finally, I felt like I lost all my energy. I decided that if my neighbor, who is Jewish, has a Jewish Scroll along the side of his door, I should put up the Holy Face plaque for a special blessing. The moment I stuck it up on my front door, I felt a power come over me, that I immediately knew I did the right thing. The power was overwhelming, not of this world. A power that I knew came directly from Christ. I was so pleased".

6.02 **God's Work**

The Holy Face office used to be located in the country. I would go to work early in the morning and then go home early to beat the rush hour traffic. One day, one of my priest friends invited me to live with him at the rectory of Our Lady of Fatima Church, in Montreal. He permitted the Holy Face Association to be located in the Church of Our Lady of Fatima.

The new spiritual director of the Holy Face Association became Father Russell Schultz. And my own spiritual director was Father Justin, a Franciscan priest. Father Russell was a tremendous help. It was always "how can I help"? He was the same with all his parishioners always saying "yes". I was very impressed with his great love for Jesus, and to know that he gave his all, no matter what. He certainly taught me a lot.

Father had a little dog called "Fodder". Of course, Fodder was the boss of the house, and everybody catered to him - but poor Fodder did not like children. This made Father Russell sad, because he liked kids so much. Fodder would not hurt the children, but he would bark at them.

My stay at Our Lady of Fatima was a very peaceful one, where we were kept busy doing our Lord's work. One day, I went to visit Father Peter Rinaldi, which I would do every few years. This time when I visited, I noticed that he had four full-length pictures of the Holy Shroud on cloth, with lights behind them. They were beautiful, and I asked if he could get some for me.

I did not know at the time why, but I knew that I must have them. When they arrived, I placed them in a tube and waited until our Lord showed me what I was to do with them.

6.03 Evangelization

In the meantime, we started different projects and called them "Holy Face Programs".

The programs were as follows:

- Holy Face Church Program
  (Lord, that we may see thy Face)
- Holy Face Home Program
  (Our Lord comes to visit his children)
- Holy Face Missionary Program
  (Go out to the whole world)
- Holy Face School Program
  (That they may learn)
- Holy Face Hospital Program
  (Our Lord consoles his children)
- Holy Face Prison Program
  (I was in prison and you visited me)

We wanted to make sure that we helped all of God's children in any way we could. We had to go to all walks of life. We had to go boldly forth to seek all of God's children. We appealed to the Blessed Mother under the title of "Our Lady of the Holy Face" and chose "The Pieta" as the image best suited for this title.

Our Lady of the Holy Face

I remember a story. One day a nun died. She came in front of the Holy Face of Jesus. On the right side of Jesus, she saw a small group of souls on the left side she saw a tremendous multitude of souls.

She asked Jesus, "Who are the small group of souls on your right"? Jesus answered, "Those are the souls you helped to get into Heaven". She then said, "Who are the tremendous multitude on the left side"? Jesus answered, "Those are the ones you could have helped".

Well, I don't want to waste time. This is the only opportunity we are given to help Jesus, in the salvation of precious souls. So precious, that God sent his only Son to come and take on our humanity and accept terrible suffering so we may all be saved. Whoever truly loves Jesus loves his children and does all in his power to help them come close to Jesus.

6.04 **The Exhibition**

You may notice that one of our projects is called the "Holy Shroud Exhibition". One day, a man came to see me who claimed to have received a message from God. He asked if I would be interested in opening a Holy Shroud Exhibition. His name was Karl Schulz. Karl was an artist, so we started to build the Holy Shroud Exhibition. When people heard what we were doing, we received help from Jerusalem to California. This help came from different priests. We also hired another artist, as well as a man to help build the showcases.

This certainly was a major undertaking, and it took approximately six months to build. We ran out of money, so I guess I made a foolish mistake by using my own credit cards so the work would continue (to this day, I still owe the money). But how can one stop such an important project; what price can you put on a soul?

Now I knew why I had ordered those four Holy Shroud pictures from Father Rinaldi (of fond memory). We had to bring this Holy Shroud Exhibition to many churches to help souls return to God in a spirit of love and reparation.

The first Exhibition was in L'Eglise du Gesù in Montreal, Canada. Wherever we went with the Exhibition, we tried to stay for one week. During the Exhibition, we seemed to always have conversions. As far as I am concerned, if we help one soul to be converted, the whole of Heaven rejoices; therefore, it will have been worthwhile to be born, for, through the grace of God, we have helped to save souls.

While I am on this subject, I would like to mention two stories: When we had the Exhibition in Toronto at the Basilica of St. Paul, Msgr. Massman was wonderful, and made sure that many people came to the Exhibition. A television interview was arranged for me at 11 o'clock in the morning. I was on my way to my car, when I felt as if someone pushed me and I fell down on the cement floor of the garage. My face was covered with blood and everyone said: "You can't go on television now" but I said that was exactly what the devil wanted.

So, off I went and when the television crew saw me, they said, "What happened to you"? I replied,

"I was in a fight and I lost but can I still go on TV"? So, I did end up on television with my message. The very next day, when I was at the Exhibition, a lady came up to me and said, "May I speak to you"? I said, "Of course", and went with her. She told me that she was from Texas, and that she had been asking herself, "What am I doing in Toronto - why am I here? I don't want to be here"!

As she was saying this, and changing television channels with the TV remote, she saw me speaking. In recounting the story to me she said, "This is why I was here; our Lord wanted me to see the Holy Shroud Exhibition. Now that I have seen the Exhibition, I am going back to Texas. I am not the same woman. I am a completely changed woman". She had been totally converted. She thanked me, and left.

Here is a second story I share here (although we have many more). There was a group of young children who had seen the Exhibition. The leader in this group of seven children (8 to 9 year olds) was a little girl. They had seen the Crown of Thorns, and the nails, etc., and we had a 4th degree Honor Guard of the Knights of Columbus, who had a sword at his side. She came up to the guard with the other children, shaking her little finger at him, asking, "Did you do this to Jesus"? Well, I have never seen a person so ill-at-ease as that guard, and the little children kept looking at him, waiting for his answer. The guard replied, "No, No! I didn't do it"! and as the children left, I heard a sigh of relief from the guard. But on second thought, each of us could have answered that question, "Yes, I did crucify Jesus". Many continue to do so. This is why much reparation is needed.

6.05 **Rejected**

One day, when I was out of town, I received an email saying that Father Schultz had a stroke. He was replaced as parish priest. When the new priest arrived, it became clear that I would have to leave and find a new place to live. We had to move the Association to new quarters. The Holy Face devotional material alone required three large trailers. The Holy Shroud Exhibition fit in one trailer.

After so many years at our Lady of Fatima Church, we were in search of a new home. The first place we found, we were told that, "We don't want you". When I asked, "Why"? the answer given was "Because you are religious". Needless to say, we looked for another place and again were told, "We don't want you". Again I asked, "Why?" Again, the answer was, "Because you are religious". The third place, we looked for lodging, we received the same response.

We had only two days to move, and were getting desperate. A friend said he knew someone who was managing a building, and would ask for his help. The manager said he would tolerate us for a short period of time, and then we would have to leave. Well, we are still here, without a lease, on a month-to-month basis.

When the Holy Face Association moved to our present address, we did not have enough room, and had to rent two additional spaces. The movers piled everything into storage without order. This frustrated us because we had a pre-arranged commitment to bring the exhibition to a major shrine in Chicago within the month and now we were in a state of disorganization.

I prayed to Jesus to help us because, at this point in time, we were in no position to fulfill our commitment. In spite of all the potential good for souls, the events were now totally beyond our control.

Within one week, I received a phone call from the priest in Chicago. He had originally asked us to bring the exhibition to his shrine, "Gordon, I have just received news of my being transferred to New York. Would you mind very much if we cancelled the exhibition, because the priest who will take my place, is not in a position to handle such a large project". I said, "Thank you Jesus".

To this present day, we are still in this building and cannot even invite one busload to come and see the Holy Shroud Exhibition. Because we would disrupt the whole building where we are, and they would probably throw us out, for they need to give just 30 days notice to do so.

We do not know when we will have a permanent home, either for the Holy Shroud Exhibition or for the Holy Face Association. We do not even know, from day to day, if we will be able to pay our rent; however, our Lord, our Blessed Mother, and St. Joseph have taken care of us for over 34 years, and continue to do so. We will continue with this work of love as long as our Heavenly Father wishes.

6.06 **Gathering of Nurses**

One day, in our new office, as I was preparing to put out a newsletter, I fell ill without warning. I was brought to the hospital for an emergency operation.

Four days after the operation, at around seven o'clock at night, I was given the opportunity to speak to a nurse about the importance of the devotion to the most Holy Face of Jesus. I closed my eyes for a few moments as I continued talking. When I reopened my eyes, I was shocked to see a group of nurses who had gathered two rows deep around my bed. They were all listening to my witness.

I knew this was a gift from God, who was showing me how his children are thirsty for his word. I asked for their addresses, and sent each of them a Holy Face medal and chain.

6.07 **Contact the Bishops**

When I was well enough to return to the office, I told Jesus that I was unable to send out the newsletter, as it was too late. Our Lord made me understand that I was to contact bishops in the western hemisphere and tell them about the importance of this devotion. When I prayed to Jesus saying that I did not have the manpower to do this, our Lord sent two Americans, a lady and her son, to help with this project in the United States. A married couple from Canada helped us contact the Canadian bishops. There was also a man and a woman from

England who helped contact the bishops in England, Wales, Scotland, and Ireland.

6.08 **Assistance at Death**

As I am the least of the least, I often tell Jesus, "Lord, have mercy on me a sinner". I cannot stress enough the importance of this devotion for not only are you protected bodily, but also, you can overcome all your interior difficulties, as was promised by your Blessed Mother. What does this mean?

You can be shown your interior weaknesses and be given the grace to overcome them. And, at the end of your life, you will die under the "Divine Gaze" of Jesus himself.

What can possibly be more important? Well, I would say that it would be nice to die under the "Divine Gaze" of Jesus and our Blessed Mother.

Now, I bring to your attention the promises of those who say the prayers of the "Seven Sorrows of our Blessed Mother".

One of the promises is that they will have our Blessed Mother present at their death.

6.09 **Financial Providence**

Although I dislike talking about money, there is something I should mention. We live a frugal life, and do not take a wage from the association (though many people think we are wealthy).

One day I ordered $60,000.00 worth of medals from Italy. Then I questioned, "What have I done because I don't have one cent in the bank"? But as God's providence would have it, within approximately one month, my cousin died without leaving a will. As her first cousin, I received an inheritance of $60,000.00 (yes), which paid the bill.

Another time, we were $40,000.00 in the red. One of our members passed away to her reward, and she left us $40,000.00 (yes).

This past year, we thought we would have to go into bankruptcy because we owed $50,000.00. A couple of weeks later, two wonderful people, Eva and Lewis, came from out of town. They said: "We knew when we came into town that we had to help someone, but we did not know who, but now we know it is you." For the love of God, they donated the $50,000.00. Truly, their reward will be great in Heaven.

To this very day, we continue operating in the red, but this Association belongs to the Lord, our Blessed Mother, and St. Joseph. I have full confidence they will continue to take care of it, and will reward all those who help in this great work for the salvation of souls.

6.10 Missionary Call

As St. Thérèse (the Little Flower) loved to help missionaries, we too strive to go all over the world to help missionaries who have given their lives to Jesus. They go to foreign lands to preach "the Word of God" and to help many come to Jesus for their salvation.

What can be more natural than to seek the face of the one you love? *"Let your face shine, that we may be saved"* (Psalm 80:7).

"Such is the company of those who seek him, who seek the face of the God of Jacob" (Psalm24:6).

Seek the Lord and be strengthened, seek his face even more. You don't hide from the face of the one you love. To refuse to gaze upon the Holy Face of Jesus implies an insult to the love and the sacrifice of the cross that brought about our redemption.

Saint Padre Pio, who bore the holy wounds of Christ crucified (the stigmata) for 50 years (1918-1968), was known to pass around Holy Face medals, with the meaningful remark: *"This is your entrance ticket to Heaven"*.

We must remember that our Lord said, *"Whoever is not with me is against me, and whoever does not gather with me scatters"* (Luke 11:23).

At baptism, you renounced the devil and his works, the world and its dissipation and sensuality. Your words are recorded not on some "monument to the dead", but in "The Book of the Living". One should not let physical desires rule one's life".

I bring to your attention what is written in one of the books of Luisa Piccarreta (known as the little daughter of the Divine Will):

"After this, my beloved Jesus transported me inside a garden in which there were many people preparing themselves to attend a feast, but only those who received a uniform were able to attend, and few were those who received this uniform. A great yearning arose in me to receive one, and I did so much that I obtained the request. So, as I reached the place in which one would receive it, a venerable matronly woman clothed me in white first, and then placed on me a pale blue shoulder band on which a medal was hanging with the imprint of the Face of Jesus. While being a Face, it was also a mirror, and in looking at it, one would detect the slightest stains, which the soul, with the help of a light coming from within that face, could easily remove. It seemed to me that that medal contained a mysterious meaning. Then she took a mantle of finest gold and covered me all over. It seemed to me that dressed in this way I could compete with the virgins in Heaven. While this was happening, Jesus told me, "*My daughter, let us go back to see what men are doing; it is enough for you to be dressed when the feast begins, I will take you there to attend*".

The following pictures from the Holy Shroud Exhibition will give you an idea of why thousands of people come to see it, and why many leave with a greater love of God, once they see how much he suffered so that they would be saved.

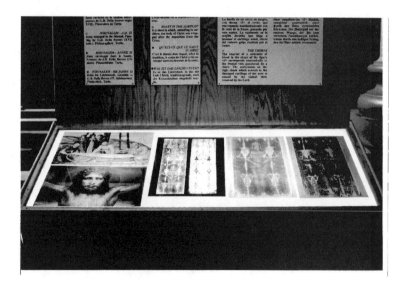

Chapter 7 - **Discovery, Journey, Destination**

Vocation to Love

Each baptized person is called to fulfill but one command: "*Love God and love your neighbor as you love yourself*" (Luke 10.27).

We are given various means by which we may succeed in this holy endeavor. While another's path may take on a different form or expression, I have chosen to follow the one briefly described in this book.

However, I am only giving what I have received. By acknowledging and receiving God's love I am made fit to embrace all those to whom he lovingly sends me.

I must respond to the question Jesus asks each one of us: "Do you love me and your neighbor"? But when I come to the end of my life, how may I be admitted to "Eternity" without carrying others in my heart?

I may not enter eternity without love for my brothers and sisters. My desire is to make the Lord better known and loved.

Do you remember the biblical story about Joseph who had been sold into slavery by his brothers? God's providence allowed him, in turn, to provide for the needs of many, not least among which were his own brothers. But, before they could be relieved of their burden and freed from their trial, they had to bring their youngest brother to Joseph.

They were told, "*You shall not see my face, unless your brother is with you*" (Genesis 43.3). In so doing, they were reminded of their sin against the law of love.

They were made free only in the company of their brother. We too are made free in the service of brothers and sisters, saints and sinners alike, whom the Lord's desire seeks to reconcile with God and with one another.

As our blessed mother said: "Tuesday is a day of reparation to the Holy Face of Jesus. We should try to go to church on tuesday and make reparation for our sins and for those who pass by a church and never go in to keep our Lord company".

I have devoted my life to promoting devotion to God by means of the image on the Shroud of Turin. This object of veneration in the Catholic Church has received both acclaim and criticism. It has opened up both scientific and theological inquiry and discussion. In the final analysis, faith's vision, guided by the Holy Spirit, penetrates the mysteries of God.

It is my hope that the image on the Shroud of Turin may deepen our understanding of the Truth of God's love for us and inspire our heartfelt response to that which we can place our complete trust – the everlasting perfection of God's love.

In response to Father McBrien's article (2009.09.08), Rev. Lawrence Farley, deacon, wrote:

This "Holy Face" - wherein is contemplated the inexhaustible love of God, is both subject and object of the devotion of "believers", be they at the public 'prayer summit' of the Mass, or along the road of their day-to-day journey, or in a chapel of adoration. Jesus Christ, truly present to us is never a "step backwards". On the contrary, to contemplate him is the central meaning of our discovery, our journey, and our destination.

The Lord calls us to live what we profess. I am reminded of an experience I had, after my conversion, when I first came back to God. I was shown that I should go to my wife and to each of my children, individually. I was to ask each one to forgive the wrongs I had done. I did this, of course, in a spirit of true sorrow.

May God allow us to continue to serve his good and kind purposes in this world, which, like the reflection on the Holy Face of Jesus - so eloquently proclaims: God is love!

AFTERWORD
By Reverend Lawrence N. Farley, p.d, sfo

The poet Gerard Manley Hopkins once said, "What you look hard at looks back hard at you".

Pope Benedict XVI says it plainly: God is the "Great Truth" who wishes to be seen.

The "Journey-Quest" portrayed throughout history in literature, on stage and screen, and visualized in art: a life called into being; a name spoken; a blessing bestowed; a finger beckoning; a challenge given; and, a decree trumpeted for a "Great Truth", which must prevail – is yours and is mine.

These stories inspire us; they belong to us collectively, and to each one personally. They appeal to our desire to detect a meaning and purpose for our existence, and to pursue happiness. And yet, if that "Great Truth" is to prevail, our happiness has bittersweet quality.

The universal appeal of "Everlasting Love" includes our collective sense that it is capable of profound suffering. This apparent contradiction is reconciled in Jesus Christ, the "Sacrificial Lamb", and made visible on his "Sacred Countenance". What is invisible is rendered visible on the journey.

However, no "Journey" is free from the burden of choice; neither does every "Discovery" find a key that opens; nor does every "Destination" end in blessed beatitude.

Jesus says, "I am the Way, the Truth and the Life" (John 14:6). With these words, Jesus speaks of the "Discovery" we are invited to make, the "Journey" we are invited to take, and the "Destination" to which we are invited to arrive.

Jesus is looking at you and me with the intensity of "Divine Love". Perhaps, when we have exhausted all our misconceptions, we may at last receive what we have looked hard at... but hardly looked at.

What will the days ahead hold for true believers? Karl Rahner, a well-known theologian, wrote, "The religious values of Christianity are being progressively eliminated from modern life, and the burden of belief is resting more and more exclusively on the personal decision of the individual".

The Holy Face of Jesus is about discovery, journey, and destination because it requires the personal decision of individuals who, like Gordon Deery, recognize what is good, and true, and holy.

Appendix A

The Novena

When I was in prayer one day in front of the Blessed Sacrament, it was made known to me that I should create a Novena of nine days in honor of the Holy Face of Jesus. This was done by much prayer and with the Power of the Holy Spirit. It took nine days to complete it.

Every day, I would compose one day of the Novena and on the ninth day, after the prayers, we said the Act of Consecration.

The Novena was to be called the "Alpha Omega Novena of the Holy Face", and it has since been shown to us by the many letters that we receive, that it is a very powerful Novena.

Our Lord said to Mother Pierina:

"See how I suffer. Nevertheless, I am understood by so few. What ingratitude on the part of those who say they love me! I have given my heart as a sensible object of my great love for man and I give my face as a sensible object of my sorrow for the sins of man".

"I desire that it be honored by a special feast on Tuesday in Quinquagesima (Shrove Tuesday, the Tuesday before Ash Wednesday). The feast will be preceded by a novena in which the faithful will make reparation with me uniting themselves with my sorrow".

Novena to the Most Holy Face of Jesus

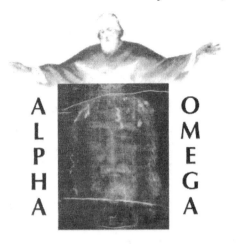

"*I firmly wish that my face reflecting the intimate pains of my soul, the suffering and love of my heart, be more honored! Whoever gazes upon me already consoles me*" (Our Lord Jesus Christ to Sister Pierina)

"*All those who, attracted by my love, and venerating my countenance, shall receive, by virtue of my humanity, a brilliant and vivid impression of my divinity. This splendor shall enlighten the depths of their souls, so that in eternal glory the celestial court shall marvel at the marked likeness of their features with my divine countenance*" (Our Lord Jesus Christ to St. Gertrude)

I now implore all the angels and saints to intercede for me as I pray this holy novena to the Most Holy Face of Jesus and for the glory of the most Holy Trinity, Father, Son and Holy Spirit. Amen.

(Start novena)

Daily Preparatory Prayer

First Day

Daily Preparatory Prayer

O Most Holy and Blessed Trinity, through the intercession of Holy Mary, whose soul was pierced through by a sword of sorrow at the sight of the passion of her Divine Son, I ask your help in making a perfect Novena of reparation with Jesus, united with all his sorrows, love and total abandonment.

Psalm 51:1-2

Have mercy on me, O God, according to your steadfast love; according to your abundant mercy blot out my transgressions. Wash me thoroughly from my iniquity, and cleanse me from my sin.

O most Holy Face of Jesus, look with tenderness on me, a sinner. You are merciful and full of love and compassion. Keep me pure of heart, so that I may see you always. Mary, my Mother, intercede for me! Saint Joseph pray for me.

Through the merits of your precious blood and your Holy Face, O Jesus, grant my petition. (.........) Grant me your pardon and mercy.

To Our Almighty Father

Almighty Father, come into my heart, and so fill me with your love that forsaking all evil desires, I may embrace you, my only good. Show me, O Lord our God, who you are for me. Say to my soul, I am your salvation, speak so that I may hear. My heart is before you; open my ears; let me hasten after your voice. Hide not your Face from me, I beseech you, O Lord. Open my heart so that you may enter in. Repair the ruined mansions that you may dwell therein. Hear me, O Heavenly Father, for the sake of your only Son, Our Lord Jesus Christ, who lives and reigns with you and the Holy Spirit, one God, now and forever. Amen. - (St. Augustine)

Our Father (1)

Hail Mary (3)

Glory Be (1)

O Bleeding Face, O Face Divine, be every adoration Thine (3)

Second Day

Daily Preparatory Prayer

O Most Holy and Blessed Trinity, through the intercession of Holy Mary, whose soul was pierced through by a sword of sorrow at the sight of the passion of her Divine Son, I ask your help in making a perfect Novena of reparation with Jesus, united with all his sorrows, love and total abandonment.

Psalm 51:3-4a

For I know my transgressions, and my sin is ever before me. Against you, you alone, have I sinned, and done what is evil in your sight.

Most Holy Face of Jesus, I am truly sorry that I have hurt you so much by constantly doing what is wrong; and for all the good works I have failed to do. Immaculate Heart of Mary and Saint Joseph intercede for me; help me to console the Most Holy Face of Jesus. Pray that I may share in the tremendous love you have for one another and for the Most Holy and Blessed Trinity. Amen.

Through the merits of your precious blood and your Holy Face, O Jesus, grant my petition. (.........) Grant me your pardon and mercy.

To the Holy Spirit

Come, Holy Spirit, Sanctifier, all powerful God of love; you who filled the Virgin Mary with grace; you who wonderfully transformed the hearts of the apostles; you who endowed all your martyrs with a miraculous heroism; come and sanctify me, illumine my mind, strengthen my will, purify my conscience, rectify my judgment, set my heart on fire and preserve me from the misfortune of resisting your inspirations. I consecrate to you my understanding, my heart and my will, my whole being for time and for eternity. May my understanding be always submissive to your heavenly inspirations and to the teachings of your Holy Catholic Church, of which you are the infallible guide; may my heart be ever inflamed with love of God and neighbor; may my will be ever conformed to the Divine Will, and may my whole life be a faithful imitation of the life and virtues of our Lord and Savior, Jesus Christ, to whom with the Father and you, the Holy Spirit, be honor and glory forever. Amen

Our Father (1)

Hail Mary (3)

Glory Be (1)

O Bleeding Face, O Face Divine, be every adoration Thine (3)

Third Day

Daily Preparatory Prayer

O Most Holy and Blessed Trinity, through the intercession of Holy Mary, whose soul was pierced through by a sword of sorrow at the sight of the passion of her Divine Son, I ask your help in making a perfect Novena of reparation with Jesus, united with all his sorrows, love and total abandonment.

Psalm 51:4b-5

You are justified in your sentence and blameless when you pass judgment. Indeed, I was born guilty, a sinner when my mother conceived me.

O Jesus! Cast upon me a look of mercy; turn your Face towards me as you did to Veronica; not that I may see it with my bodily eyes, for this I do not deserve, but turn it towards my heart, so that, remembering you, I may ever draw from this fountain of strength the vigor necessary to sustain the combats of life. Amen. Mary, my Mother, and Saint Joseph, pray for me. – *(Pope Pius IX)*

Through the merits of your precious blood and your Holy Face, O Jesus, grant my petition. (.........) Grant me your pardon and mercy.

All highest, glorious God, cast your light into the darkness of my heart, give me true faith, firm hope, perfect charity and profound humility, so that with wisdom, courage and perception, O Lord, I may do what is truly your holy will. Amen – *(Saint Francis)*

To the Angels and Saints

I salute you, through the Holy Face and Sacred Heart of Jesus, O all you holy angels and saints of God. I rejoice in your glory, and I give thanks to our Lord for all the benefits, which he has showered upon you; I praise him, and glorify him, and offer to you, for an increase of your joy and honor, the most Holy Face and gentle Heart of Jesus. Pray that I may become formed according to the Heart of Jesus. Amen.

Our Father (1)

Hail Mary (3)

Glory Be (1)

O Bleeding Face, O Face Divine, be every adoration Thine (3)

Fourth Day

Daily Preparatory Prayer

O Most Holy and Blessed Trinity, through the intercession of Holy Mary, whose soul was pierced through by a sword of sorrow at the sight of the passion of her Divine Son, I ask your help in making a perfect Novena of reparation with Jesus, united with all his sorrows, love and total abandonment.

Psalm 51:6-7

You desire truth in the inward being; therefore teach me wisdom in my secret heart. Purge me with hyssop, and I shall be clean; wash me, and I shall be whiter than snow.

O Lord Jesus, who has said, "*Learn of me for I am meek and gentle of heart*", and who manifested upon your Holy Face the sentiments of your Divine Heart, grant that I may love to come frequently and meditate upon your divine features. I may read there your gentleness and your humility, and learn how to form my heart in the practice of these two virtues, which you desire to see shine in your servants. Mary, our Mother, intercede for me! Saint Joseph pray for me.

Through the merits of your precious blood and your Holy Face, O Jesus, grant my petition. (.........) Grant me your pardon and mercy.

In Honor of the Sorrows of the Blessed Virgin

O Most Holy and afflicted Virgin, Queen of Martyrs, who stood beneath the cross, witnessing the agony of your dying Son, look down with a mother's tenderness and pity on me as I kneel before you to venerate your sorrows, and place my requests, with filial confidence, in the sanctuary of your wounded heart. Present them on my behalf to Jesus, through the merits of his most sacred passion and death, together with the sufferings of your sorrowful heart at the foot of the cross; and through the unity of both, obtain the favor, which I humbly request. To whom shall I go in my needs and misery if not to you? O Mother of Mercy, having so deeply drunk of the chalice of your Son, graciously ease the sufferings of those who still sigh in this land of exile. Amen.

For the Souls in Purgatory

My Jesus, by the sorrows you suffered in your agony in the garden, in your scourging and crowning with thorns, in the way to Calvary, in your crucifixion and death, have mercy on the souls in Purgatory, and especially on those that are most forsaken. Deliver them from the dire torments they endure. Call them and admit them to your most sweet embrace in paradise. Amen.

Our Father (1)

Hail Mary (3)

Glory Be (1)

O Bleeding Face, O Face Divine, be every adoration Thine (3)

Fifth Day

Daily Preparatory Prayer

O Most Holy and Blessed Trinity, through the intercession of Holy Mary, whose soul was pierced through by a sword of sorrow at the sight of the passion of her Divine Son, I ask your help in making a perfect Novena of reparation with Jesus, united with all his sorrows, love and total abandonment.

Psalm 51:8-9

Let me hear joy and gladness; let the bones that you have crushed rejoice. Hide your face from my sins, and blot out all my iniquities.

Holy Face of Jesus, Sacred Countenance of God, how great is your patience with humankind, how infinite your forgiveness! I am a sinner, yet you still love me. This gives us courage. For the glory of your Holy Face and of the Blessed Trinity, hear and answer us. Mary, our Mother, intercede for me! Saint Joseph pray for me.

Through the merits of your precious blood and your Holy Face, O Jesus, grant my petition. (.........) Grant me your pardon and mercy.

To Saint Joseph

Dear Saint Joseph, adopt me as your child; take charge of my salvation; watch over me day and night; preserve me from the occasions of sin; obtain for me purity of body and soul, and the spirit of prayer, through your intercession with Jesus; grant me a spirit of sacrifice, of humility and self-denial; obtain for me a burning love for Jesus in the Blessed

Sacrament, and a sweet and tender love for Mary, our Mother. Saint Joseph, be with me in life and in death, and obtain for me a favorable judgment from Jesus, my merciful Savior. Amen.

Our Father (1)

Hail Mary (3)

Glory Be (1)

O Bleeding Face, O Face Divine, be every adoration Thine (3)

Sixth Day

Daily Preparatory Prayer

O Most Holy and Blessed Trinity, through the intercession of Holy Mary, whose soul was pierced through by a sword of sorrow at the sight of the passion of her Divine Son, I ask your help in making a perfect Novena of reparation with Jesus, united with all his sorrows, love and total abandonment.

Psalm 51:10-11

Create in me a clean heart, O God, and put a new and right spirit within me. Do not cast me away from your presence, and do not take your holy spirit from me.

May my heart be cleansed, O Lord, by the inpouring of the Holy Spirit. May he make it fruitful by watering it with his heavenly dew. Mary, the most chaste spouse of the Holy Spirit, intercede for me, Saint Joseph pray for me.

Through the merits of your precious blood and your Holy Face, O Jesus, grant my petition. (.........) Grant me your pardon and mercy.

To Saint Michael the Archangel

O Victorious Prince, most humble guardian of the Church of God and of faithful souls, who with such charity and zeal takes part in so many conflicts and gains such great victories over the enemy, for the conservation and protection of the honor and glory we all owe to God, as well as for the promotion of our salvation; come, I pray you, to my assistance, for I am continually besieged with such great perils by my enemies - the flesh, the world, and the devil; and, as you were a leader for the people of God through their desert journey, so also be my faithful leader and companion through the desert of this world, until you conduct me safely into the happy land of the living, in that blessed Fatherland from which we are all exiles. Amen. *(St. Aloysius)*

Our Father (1)

Hail Mary (3)

Glory Be (1)

O Bleeding Face, O Face Divine, be every adoration Thine (3)

Seventh Day

Daily Preparatory Prayer

O Most Holy and Blessed Trinity, through the intercession of Holy Mary, whose soul was pierced through by a sword of sorrow at the sight of the passion of her Divine Son, I ask your help in making a perfect Novena of reparation with Jesus, united with all his sorrows, love and total abandonment.

Psalm 51:12-13

Restore to me the joy of your salvation, and sustain in me a willing spirit. Then I will teach transgressors your ways, and sinners will return to you.

Lord Jesus, after contemplating your features, disfigured by grief; after meditating upon your passion with compunction and love, how can my heart fail to be inflamed with a holy hatred of sin, which even now outrages your adorable Face!

Lord, suffer me not to be content with mere compassion, but give me the grace, so closely to follow you, in this Calvary, so that the disrespect destined for you may fall on me.

O Jesus, in this way I have a share, small though it may be, in the expiation of sin. Amen. Mary, our Mother, intercede for me! Saint Joseph pray for me.

Through the merits of your precious blood and your Holy Face, O Jesus, grant my petition. (.........) Grant me your pardon and mercy.

In Honor of Mary

Hail Mary, Daughter of God the Father! Hail Mary, Mother of God the Son! Hail Mary, Spouse of the Holy Spirit! Hail Mary, Temple of the Most Holy Trinity! Hail Mary, my mistress, my wealth, my mystic rose, Queen of my heart, my Mother, my life, my sweetness, and my dearest hope! I am all yours, and all I have is yours. O Virgin blessed above all things, may your soul be in me to magnify the Lord; may your spirit be in me to rejoice in God. Place yourself, O faithful Virgin, as a seal upon my heart, that in you and through you, I may be found faithful to God. Grant, most gracious Virgin, that I may be numbered among those whom you are pleased to love, to teach and to guide, to favor and to protect as your child. Grant that with the help of your love, I may despise all earthly consolation and cling to heavenly things, until through the Holy Spirit, your faithful spouse, and through you, his faithful spouse, Jesus Christ, your Son, be formed within me for the glory of the Father. Amen. – *(St. Grignon de Montfort)*

Our Father (1)

Hail Mary (3)

Glory Be (1)

O Bleeding Face, O Face Divine, be every adoration Thine (3)

Eighth Day

Daily Preparatory Prayer

O Most Holy and Blessed Trinity, through the intercession of Holy Mary, whose soul was pierced through by a sword of sorrow at the sight of the passion of her Divine Son, I ask your help in making a perfect Novena of reparation with Jesus, united with all his sorrows, love and total abandonment.

Psalm 51:14-15

Deliver me from bloodshed, O God, O God of my salvation, and my tongue will sing aloud of your deliverance. O Lord, open my lips, and my mouth will declare your praise.

Most merciful Face of Jesus, who in this vale of tears was so moved by our misfortunes to call yourself the healer of the sick, and the Good Shepherd of the souls gone astray, allow not Satan to draw me away from you, but keep me always under your loving protection, together with all souls who endeavor to console you. Mary, my Mother, intercede for me! Saint Joseph pray for me.

Through the merits of your precious blood and your Holy Face, O Jesus, grant my petition. (.........) Grant me your pardon and mercy.

To Saint Peter

O glorious Saint Peter, in return for your lively and generous faith, your profound and sincere humility, and your burning love, you were honored by Jesus Christ with singular privileges; and in particular, with the leadership of the other apostles and the primacy of the whole church, of which you were made the foundation stone - obtain for me the grace of a lively faith, that shall not fear to profess itself openly, in its entirety and in all of its manifestations, even to the shedding of blood, if occasion should demand it; and to the sacrifice of life itself in preference to surrender. Obtain for me, likewise, a sincere loyalty to our Holy Mother the Church. Grant that I may ever remain most closely and sincerely united to the Holy Father, who is the heir of your faith and of your authority, the one true visible head of the Catholic Church. Grant, moreover, that I may follow, in all humility and meekness, the Church's teaching and counsels and may be obedient to all her precepts, in order to be able here on earth to enjoy a peace that is sure and undisturbed, and to attain one day in heaven to everlasting happiness. Amen.

Our Father (1)

Hail Mary (3)

Glory Be (1)

O Bleeding Face, O Face Divine, be every adoration Thine (3)

Ninth Day

Daily Preparatory Prayer

O Most Holy and Blessed Trinity, through the intercession of Holy Mary, whose soul was pierced through by a sword of sorrow at the sight of the passion of her Divine Son, I ask your help in making a perfect Novena of reparation with Jesus, united with all his sorrows, love and total abandonment.

Psalm 51:16-19

For you have no delight in sacrifice; if I were to give a burnt offering, you would not be pleased. The sacrifice acceptable to God is a broken spirit; a broken and contrite heart, O God, you will not despise. Do good to Zion in your good pleasure; rebuild the walls of Jerusalem, then you will delight in right sacrifices, in burnt offerings and whole burnt offerings; then bulls will be offered on your altar.

Sacred Face of my Lord and my God, what words can I use to express my gratitude? How can I speak of the joy, which you graciously grant to me, and which you have decided to answer in my hour of need? I say this because I know that my prayers will be granted. I know that you have listened to my pleading heart, and, in your loving kindness, will grant the answer to my problems. Mary, my Mother, thank you for your intercession on my behalf. Saint Joseph, thank you for your prayers.

Through the merits of your precious blood and your Holy Face, O Jesus, grant my petition. (.........) Grant me your pardon and mercy.

To the Holy Trinity

Most Holy Trinity, Godhead indivisible, Father, Son, and Holy Spirit, my first beginning and my last end: since you have made me after your own image and likeness, grant that all the thoughts of my mind, all the words I speak, all the affections of my heart and all my actions may be always conformed to your most Holy Will, so that after having seen you here on earth in appearances and rather dimly, through the means of faith, I may come at last to contemplate you face to face, in the perfect possession of you forever in paradise. Amen.

Our Father (1)

Hail Mary (3)

Glory Be (1)

O Bleeding Face, O Face Divine, be every adoration Thine (3)

Personal Consecration To Jesus Christ

Tenth Day

Act of Consecration

O Lord Jesus, I believe most firmly in you. I love you. You are the Eternal Son of God and the Son Incarnate of the Blessed Virgin Mary. You are the Lord and Absolute Ruler of all creation.

I acknowledge you, therefore, as the Universal Sovereign of all creatures. You are the Lord and Supreme Ruler of all mankind, and I, in acknowledging this your dominion, consecrate myself to you, now and forever.

Loving Jesus, I place my family under the protection of your Holy Face, and of your Virgin Mother, Mary most sorrowful. I promise to be faithful to you for the rest of my life and to observe with fidelity your Holy Commandments.

Before others, I will never deny you or your divine rights over me. Grant me the grace to never sin again; nevertheless, should I fail, O Divine Savior, have mercy on me and restore me to your grace.

Radiate your Divine Countenance upon me, and bless me now and forever. Through the intercession of your Blessed Mother, of all your saints who behold you in heaven and the just who glorify you on earth, embrace me at the hour of death, and bring me into your Kingdom for all eternity.

O Jesus, be mindful of me forever and never forsake me - protect my family.

O Mother of Sorrows, by the eternal glory that you enjoy in heaven, through the merits of your bitter anguish in the Sacred Passion of your Beloved Son, our Lord Jesus Christ - obtain for me the grace that the Precious Blood, shed by Jesus for the redemption of souls, be not shed in vain for me. I love you, O Mary. Embrace me and bless me, O Mother. Protect me in life and in death. Amen.

Glory Be (1)

Note

- Devotion to the Holy Face should be associated with the "Consecration of Homes to Jesus". This was confirmed by Saint Pius X.

- "Tuesday" is a day of reparation to the Holy Face (preferably before the Blessed Sacrament in the tabernacle). Our Blessed Mother revealed this to Sister Pierina.

- Wearing a blessed medal or a Holy Face scapular around one's neck (till death) is the best way to complete the consecration.

One side of the traditional medal (or scapular) has the image of the Holy Face; while the other side, has the image of the Blessed Sacrament.

To gain the blessings promised one must demonstrate faith.

Appendix B

Render Your Thanksgiving

Dear H.F.A.

"Thank you for the Holy Face Medals and accompanying leaflets and also the additional leaflets you enclosed. I have a peace and calm, the likes of which I have never known since wearing the medal and distributing it. Furthermore, I have received inestimable graces and blessings. May God bless you abundantly, and may he guard you always". – Margaret (Seattle, Washington)

Dear H.F.A.

"I was moved to send for a Holy Face medal. Four days after wearing this medal, I was filled with a peace and joy that I know comes only from God. After fighting depression for three years, this was the completion of my healing. The peace and joy have not left me. I am smiling all the time. God Bless you all" - L. Jones (California)

Dear H.F.A.

"Wearing the Holy Face medal and praying to Jesus every day sure makes a difference. I wish I had done this years ago! I know what the Holy Face of Jesus has done for me since April when I started to wear the medal. Thank you so much"! - George (Ontario, Canada)

Dear H.F.A.

"You would cry to see the poverty, misery and suffering here - but you must see the happiness and joy on the faces of those who receive the Holy Face medal. We have many conversions, cures, and healings. Please continue to help us. You and the Holy Face Association members are in our Masses and prayers". - Father G. Janson (S. India)

Dear H.F.A.

"I have become interested in the devotion to the Holy Face of Jesus since reading "The Treasure of the Holy Face of Jesus" book. I would appreciate you sending me the list of items available. Thank you very much". – Ann (New York)

Dear H.F.A.

"Hi! I just thought I would let you know that the class I taught using the Holy Face items you supplied was amazing! Every one of my Fourth Graders was spellbound, and couldn't wait to share the things they learned with their families! I truly believe that the lesson has strengthened their faith. It was an amazing thing to see. Thanks again for the opportunity to teach a lesson that the class will never forget." - Mrs. Michelle (Battle Creek)

Dear H.F.A.

Thanks a lot for the newsletter. A beautiful write-up! I was greatly touched by its contents. It made me feel guilty because I immediately saw myself as one of those that have been fighting and silently saying no to the calling of the Lord. Thank you for lifting up my spirit, and reinvigorating my confidence in God. I am asking our Lord also to run my life and to take away from my heart the fear of the unknown. Thanks for your unquantifiable blessing. Your write-up has aroused a deep love in my heart for the Holy Face of Jesus. - Grace (Canada)

Dear H.F.A.
"To whom it may concern: I am writing to let you know my son has experienced a miracle. I have been praying for him for over 25 years. He suffers from Post-Traumatic Stress. I have recited the 9-day Alpha - Omega Holy Face Novena each day from start to finish. My son told me that he has received the Holy Spirit. I thank God, our Father, for this great gift of salvation! I trust in Jesus, he has won the victory". – Jennie (New Jersey)

Dear H.F.A.
The Lord is with us as I write this letter, and always. I thank God and you for the powerful faith given me in our Lord, as a consequence of wearing my medal. With thanks and warmest regards. - John K. (USA)

Dear H.F.A.
"I must tell you that a lady I gave a leaflet and one medal to returned to the Sacraments after being away for twenty nine years. Also, a man (an alcoholic) has stopped drinking, thanks to the Holy Face". – Catherine (Florida)

Dear H.F.A.
Today, I received your exceedingly kind letter of June 27th. Very sincerely I thank you for it. I could see in it your overflowing devotion to the Holy Face. What a joy you find in seeing others growing in their devotion to the Holy Face! I believe that the Holy Face picture and medal are very merciful gifts of the good Lord to save perishing humanity.

The picture and medal are so helpful to enkindle faith and love even in the most depraved. So I always carry in my pocket a few Holy Face pictures and medals, so that I may be able to instill devotion to them, in anyone with whom I come in contact. As I am a retreat preacher, I make use of every opportunity to speak of the Holy Face in my retreat talks. I find that impresses the Retreat members most.

The leaflet about the redeeming power of the Mass, as preached by Fr. Mateo, SS.CC, deeply touched me. I find it highly helpful to deepen devotion to the Holy Eucharist. So kindly send me a number of these leaflets. With very loving regards, and in union of prayers, ever devotedly yours in the Holy Face. - Father John, O.I.C.

Dear H.F.A.
"My life has changed dramatically since I have brought God into my life. I realize now why we are here on earth and what there is to live for. Thank you so much! I feel I must let others see the goodness through my happiness. Once again thank you so much for helping me"! – Pamela (USA)

Dear H.F.A.
I had surgery, and the medicine they gave me for my kidneys was excruciatingly painful. So I applied the Holy Face oil to my side. Oh my gosh! It was as if someone pulled the plug! I came into the next room and told my son Filip that "I applied the holy oil and that the spasms went away immediately". My thanks to you, Jesus! - Halina & Fillip

Dear H.F.A.

Will you please send me some Holy Face prayers and medals to give to others? I have one and have greatly benefited an immediate conversion and am now very strong in faith. Love in God. - Joan C. (USA)

Dear H.F.A.

Please send me 10 medals of the Holy Face. At one time, I had a plaque of the Holy Face, which was adhered to my front door. It was lost during the Hurricane. (I was the only apartment that was not flooded! Praise God.) Do you still have these? Please let me know, as I would like to order one. Also please send me one Holy Face Scapular and one Our Lady of Mt. Carmel Scapular. Thank you! - Dorothy

Dear H.F.A.

Recently, I have received the Holy Face medal. Ever since, my life has been enlightened and I have a wonderful feeling of peace deep inside my heart. I wish to thank you for providing people with the opportunity to receive and wear this Blessing. Please also send 100 Holy Face leaflets. Thank you again and keep up the good work. - Brian, P.A. (USA)

Dear H.F.A.

"This Alpha-Omega Novena has brought us comfort at very stressful times and many blessings and healing". Love in Jesus' name, - Anna & Walter (New Orleans, USA)

Dear H.F.A.

I received a Blessed medal of the Holy Face of Jesus and experienced a real miracle! For nearly a year, I have had a polyp in the back of my throat that had been examined by a doctor. When I received the

Blessed medal, I really felt that the Lord had told me to hold the Blessed medal up to my mouth, and let the Face of Jesus show upon the back of my throat. I know this all sounds fantastic, but the next morning when I awoke, the polyp was gone. Thanks again for your ministry and God Bless you! - Brent (Alabama)

Dear H.F.A.

I am writing this letter to thank you with all my heart for the medals that you have given me. These medals have given us so many graces, it's unbelievable! My Auntie Carmen had cancer and the medal of the Sacred Face of Jesus cured her. I am so grateful. God Bless you. All my love. - Doreen (Australia)

Dear H.F.A.

I never prayed a novena before, until my friend presented me with the Holy Face of Jesus. I did not believe I was worthy enough for Jesus to love and forgive me for all my transgressions, or that it would work for me; however, since I have been carrying out my devotions daily and wearing the medal, I have found such peace and joy. I would like to give one to my mother who is extremely ill. I would like her to find the same peace and joy I have found, and I would also like to share one with my girlfriend. Thank you for your prompt attention; and may God bless you all! Sincerely, - Sonia, (Santa Barbara, CA. USA)

Dear H.F.A.

"Thank you so much for the leaflets, especially the three medals. Ever since I started wearing it, a lot of happy "unexplained" things have happened to me. I never felt alone ever since I started wearing it. My faith grew stronger and I can say that the heavens already showed me a miracle I will never forget. GOD Bless! You'll always be in my prayers forever"! Love, - May (NY, USA)

Dear H.F.A.
A man called David, came over from Ireland with terminal cancer, and he went to the hospital in Birmingham to see if anything could be done for him. Someone gave him a Holy Face medal, and when he went back for the results for the tests that had been taken, they found him completely cured! David was so relieved that he took 250 of your medals back to Ireland to give to his friends. This is about a family who didn't speak for more than 20 years because of a family feud. Again one man who took ill was given the Holy Face medal. Within days all the family (nieces, nephews, etc) came to see him and they all got on really well. Not one of them mentioned the feud! The power of the Holy Face is really remarkable. Take care, and God bless! – Gloria (U.K.)

Dear H.F.A.
"Thank you so much for the wonderful prayer book, *The Treasure of the Holy Face of Jesus*'. I find this book gives me much faith, hope and inspiration in my daily prayers". - Michelle (Canada)

Dear H.F.A
"I stumbled across your organization about a year ago. It was a really rough time in my life. Things in my life were falling apart. I sent off for one of the holy Face medals and when I received it, things turned around like a light shining into the darkest night. It has restored my faith in Jesus, and God has proved His love for me ever since. I bought 100 of the medals and gave them to every one of my friends and

relatives. I tell everyone I get a chance to, about the H.F.A. and I spread the word about the Holy Face of Jesus Christ. I thank God every day for what He has done for me! I have dedicated my life to sharing the word of God and the devotion to the Holy Face of Jesus. He is the love of my life. Thank you for helping me restore my faith". Your brother in Christ, - Keith

Appendix C

Pray, Pray, Pray
Love God with all your heart, and soul, and mind…
Love your neighbor as yourself. – Mt. 22:36

Prayer to the Holy Spirit

O Holy Spirit, in these days of doubt, confusion, and uncertainty, come into our hearts with your light, your strength, and your consolation.

Come with the light of truth and teach us the will of God in our daily living; especially now when God's basic laws are challenged or ignored.

Come with your strength that purifies our heart and our desires and guards us against the danger of pride and self–conceit.

Bring your consolation so that with a heart attuned to your holy love, we may live in peace and harmony in our families and give to our communities the spirit of cooperation, tolerance, and understanding.

O God, you have instructed the faithful with the light of the Holy Spirit. Grant that through this same Holy Spirit we may be truly wise and enjoy his consolation always. Amen.

Prayer at the consecration
(As the priest begins to consecrate the bread and wine)
O Holy Spirit, when the priest calls upon you to change the bread and wine into the body and blood of Jesus, I call upon you to change our hearts and make them pleasing to you.

The Fatima Prayers
My God, I believe, I adore, I trust, and I love you. I beg pardon for those who do not believe, do not adore, do not trust, and do not love you. Amen.

Most Holy Trinity, Father, Son and Holy Spirit, I adore you profoundly, and I offer you the most precious Body, Blood, Soul and Divinity of Jesus Christ, present in all tabernacles of the world, in reparation for the sacrileges, outrages and indifference by which he is offended; and by the infinite merits of his most Sacred Heart, and through the intercession of the Immaculate Heart of Mary, I beg the conversion of poor sinners. Amen.

The Memorare Prayer
Remember, O most gracious Virgin Mary, that never was it known that anyone who fled to your protection, implored your help, or sought your intercession was left unaided. Inspired by this confidence, I fly unto you, O Virgin of virgins, my mother; to you do I come, before you I stand, sinful and sorrowful. O Mother of the Word Incarnate despise not my petitions, but in your mercy, hear and answer me. Amen.

O Salutaris Hostia
O salutaris Hostia, Quae caeli pandis ostium:
Bella premunt hostilia, Da robur, fer auxilium.
Uni trinoque Domino Sit sempiterna gloria,
Qui vitam sine termino
Nobis donet in patria. Amen.

(English version)
O saving Victim, opening wide

The gate of heaven to all us below:
Our foes press on from every side;
Thine aid supply, Thy strength bestow.
To Thy great Name be endless praise,
Immortal Godhead, One in Three!
O grant us endless length of days
With Thee in our true country. Amen.

To St. Michael the Archangel

St. Michael the Archangel, defend us in battle; be our defense against the wickedness and snares of the Devil. May God restrain him, we humbly pray; and do you, O Prince of the Heavenly Host, by the Power of God, cast into hell Satan and all the other evil spirits, who prowl about the world, seeking the ruin of souls. Amen.

Tantum Ergo

Tantum ergo Sacramentum
veneremur cernui:
et antiquum documentum
novo cedat ritui:
praestet fides supplementum
sensuum defectui.
Genitori, Genitoque laus et iubilatio, salus, honor,
virtus quoque sit et benedictio: procedenti ab
utroque compar sit laudatio. Amen.

(English version)
Down in adoration falling,
Lo! the sacred Host we hail;
Lo! o'er ancient forms departing,
newer rites of grace prevail;
faith for all defects supplying,
where the feeble senses fail.

To the everlasting Father, and the Son who reigns on high, with the Holy Ghost proceeding forth from each eternally, be salvation, honor, blessing, might and endless majesty. Amen.

Prayer for the Vicar of Christ (the Pope)
(Roman Ritual)
Lord, source of eternal life and truth, give to your shepherd, the Pope, a spirit of courage and right judgment, a spirit of knowledge and love. By governing with fidelity those entrusted to his care may he, as successor to the apostle Peter and Vicar of Christ, build your church into a sacrament of unity, love, and peace for the whole world. We ask this through our Lord Jesus Christ, Your Son, who lives and reigns with you and the Holy Spirit, one God, forever and ever. Amen.

Litany of the Holy Face
In the words of our Lord Jesus Christ to Sister Pierina, *"I firmly wish that my face reflecting the intimate pains of my soul, the suffering and love of my heart, be more honored! Whoever gazes upon me already consoles me."*

V. Lord, have mercy on us,
R. *Lord, have mercy on us.*

V. Christ, have mercy on us,
R. *Christ, have mercy on us.*

V. Lord, have mercy on us,
R. *Lord, have mercy on us.*

V. Christ, hear us,
R. *Christ, graciously hear us.*

V. God, the Father in Heaven,
R. *Have mercy on us.*

V. God, the Son, Redeemer of the world,
R. *Have mercy on us.*

V. God, the Holy Spirit,
R. *Have mercy on us.*

V. Holy Trinity, One God,
R. *Have mercy on us.*

Adorable Face of Jesus, masterpiece of the Holy Spirit.
(Save us)

Adorable Face of Jesus, perfect image of the humanity of Mary
(Save us)

Adorable Face of Jesus, everlasting joy in the sight of Mary and Joseph.
(Save us)

Adorable Face of Jesus, adored by the Angels in Bethlehem.
(Save us)

Adorable Face of Jesus, splendor of the Holy Family.
(Save us)

Adorable Face of Jesus, vanquisher of demons.
(Save us)

Adorable Face of Jesus, consoling relief of sinners.
(Save us)

Adorable Face of Jesus, gentle relief of the burdened.
(Save us)

Adorable Face of Jesus, affirmer of brotherly charity.
(Save us)

Adorable Face of Jesus, shining like the sun on Mount Thabor.
(Save us)

Adorable Face of Jesus, resplendent joy of the Apostles.

(Save us)

Adorable Face of Jesus, bowed to the ground in the Garden of Gethsemane.

(Save us)

Adorable Face of Jesus, whose glance caused Peter to weep bitterly.

(Save us)

Adorable Face of Jesus, covered, struck and taunted in the brutal buffeting.

(Save us)

Adorable Face of Jesus, covered with spittle from vile mouths. *(Save us)*

Adorable Face of Jesus, whose head was crowned with thorns and struck with a reed.

(Save us)

Adorable Face of Jesus, taunted in the horrible agony.

(Save us)

Adorable Face of Jesus, praying for your executioners.

(Save us)

Adorable Face of Jesus, whose pitiable sight grieved the Mother of Sorrows.

(Save us)

Adorable Face of Jesus, veiled in the pallor of death.

(Save us)

Adorable Face of Jesus, imprinted on the Holy Shroud.

(Save us)

Adorable Face of Jesus, resplendent on Easter Morning.

(Save us)

Adorable Face of Jesus, radiant in the Ascension.

(Save us)

Adorable Face of Jesus, Splendor of Paradise.

(Save us)

Adorable Face of Jesus, adoration of the Angels.

(Save us)

Adorable Face of Jesus, everlasting joy of the Saints.

(Save us)

Adorable Face of Jesus, calling the Elect to Eternal Glory.

(Save us)

Adorable Face of Jesus, veiled in the Adorable Sacrament of the Altar.

(Save us)

Lamb of God, who takes away the sins of the world.

(Spare us, O Lord)

Lamb of God, who takes away the sins of the world.

(Graciously hear us, O Lord)

Lamb of God, who takes away the sins of the world.

(Have mercy on us)

V. Lord, show us your Face.
R. And we shall be saved.

Let us pray:
Eternal Father, through the Immaculate Heart of Mary, we offer you the Holy Face of Jesus.

May we who meditate on the countenance of your Son, be a consoling influence in His body the Church.

May we profit from the merits of His passion, death and resurrection.

And may we be found worthy to walk in the way of the cross. Amen.

Prayer to Our Lady of Seven Sorrows

The Blessed Virgin Mary grants seven graces to the souls who honor her daily by meditating on her tears and sorrows. The Hail Mary is prayed seven times, once after each meditation. St. Bridget passed on this devotion.

The seven sorrows of our Lady:
1. The prophecy of Simeon (Lk. 2.34-35).
2. Holy Family's flight into Egypt (Mt. 2.13-14).
3. Loss of child Jesus in the Temple (Lk. 2.43-45).
4. Jesus meeting Mary on the Way of the Cross.
5. The crucifixion and death of Jesus.
6. Taking down Jesus' body from the cross.
7. The burial of Jesus in the tomb.

The seven graces to souls who meditate the sorrows:
1. I will grant peace to their families.
2. They will be enlightened about the divine mysteries.
3. I will console them in their pains and I will accompany them in their work.
4. I will give them as much as they ask for as long as it does not oppose the adorable will of my divine Son or the sanctification of their souls.
5. I will defend them in their spiritual battles with the infernal enemy and I will protect them at every instant of their lives.
6. I will visibly help them at the moment of their death; they will see the face of their Mother.
7. I have obtained (this grace) from my divine Son, that those who propagate this devotion to my tears and sorrows, will be taken directly from this earthly life to eternal happiness since all their sins will be forgiven and my Son and I will be their eternal consolation and joy.

The Golden Arrow Prayer
(as dictated by Our Lord to Sister Marie of St. Peter)

May the most holy, most sacred, most adorable, most incomprehensible and ineffable Name of God be forever praised, blessed, loved, adored and glorified in heaven, on earth, and under the earth by all the creatures of God and by the Sacred Heart of Our Lord Jesus Christ in the Most Holy Sacrament of the Altar. Amen.

Eternal Father, I offer thee the adorable Face of thy Beloved Son for the honor and glory of thy name, for the conversion of sinners and the salvation of the dying. Amen.

SOURCES AND REFERENCES

Decree of the Congregation for the Causes of Saints. April 3, 2009. Venerable Servant of God Maria Pierina de Micheli, Italian sister of the Daughters of the Immaculate Conception of Buenos Aires, (online): http://ihmhermitage.stblogs.com/2009/04/03/decrees-of-the-congregation-for-the-causes-of-saints-6/ (accessed February 1, 2010).

Deery, Gordon. *The Treasure of the Holy Face of Jesus*, 31. Montréal, Québec, Canada: Imprimerie Transnumérique Inc. 1993.

Deery, Gordon. "O Salutaris" *The Treasure of the Holy Face of Jesus*, 31. Montréal, Québec, Canada: Imprimerie Transnumérique Inc. 1993.

Deery, Gordon. "Litany of the Holy Face" *The Treasure of the Holy Face of Jesus*, 32-35. Montréal, Québec, Canada: Imprimerie Transnumérique Inc. 1993.

Deery, Gordon. "Divine Praises" *The Treasure of the Holy Face of Jesus*, 44. Montréal, Québec, Canada: Imprimerie Transnumérique Inc. 1993.

Deery, Gordon. "Tantum Ergo" *The Treasure of the Holy Face of Jesus*, 44. Montréal, Québec, Canada: Imprimerie Transnumérique Inc. 1993.

Deery, Gordon. "Act of Contrition" *The Treasure of the Holy Face of Jesus*, 56. Montréal, Québec, Canada: Imprimerie Transnumérique Inc. 1993.

Deery, Gordon. "St. Michael" *The Treasure of the Holy Face of Jesus*, 57. Montréal, Québec, Canada: Imprimerie Transnumérique Inc. 1993.

Deery, Gordon. "For the Pope" *The Treasure of the Holy Face of Jesus*, 61. Montréal, Québec, Canada: Imprimerie Transnumérique Inc. 1993.

Deery, Gordon. "Memorare" *The Treasure of the Holy Face of Jesus*, 64. Montréal, Québec, Canada: Imprimerie Transnumérique Inc. 1993.

Discalced Carmalite Nuns, at Tours. "The Autobiography and Revelations of Sister Mary of St. Peter" *The Golden Arrow*. 3rd ed. by Dorothy Scallan. Tan Publishers, 1990.

Father Richard McBrien, "Perpetual eucharistic adoration", posted in the online version of the National Catholic Reporter, http://ncronline.org/blogs/essays-theology/perpetual-eucharistic-adoration (accessed September 29, 2009).

Frederic and Mary Ann Brussat, review of *Hope Against Darkness*, by Richard Rohr, John Bookster Feister, St. Anthony Messenger Press (December 2000), http://www.spiritualityandpractice.com/books/books.php?id=2662 (accessed October 5, 2009)

Janvier, M. L'Abbe. *Life of Sister Mary of St. Peter, Carmelite of Tours*. 388. Washington, D.C., Office of the Librarian of Congress, revised ed., 1884. http://www.archive.org/stream/lifeofsistermary00janvuoft#page/n3/mode/2up (accessed August 10, 2009)

Karl Rahner, "Sacred Heart", The Eternal Year, trans. John Shea, S. S. (London: Burns and Oates, 1964)

Marciano Baptsta, The Devotion Of The Future According To Karl Rahner", Theology Annual, vol. 4, 1980, p.149-165. http://www.xhchina.org/sxnk/annaul/A004i.htm (accessed October 7, 2009)

Martins, Cardinal José Saraiva. "The Face of Christ in the Face of the Church". http://www.vatican.va/roman_curia/congregations/csaints/documents/rc_con_csaints_doc_20021210_martins-rosto-de-cristo_en.html (accessed April 19, 2009).

Meditations from Carmel, "Revealed to and quoted by Sister
Marie St. Pierre, Carmelite",
http://www.meditationsfromcarmel.com/holy_face.html
(accessed October 5, 2009)

Moser, Barry. *In the Face of Presumption.* USA, Godine, 2000:
Tenakh & Testament, 174.

NRSV (online): biblical quotes at Crosswalk Bible Study Tools,
www.biblestudytools.com/nrs/ (accessed May 5, 2009).

NRSV (online): biblical quotes accessed at Bible Study Tools,
www.biblestudytools.com/nrs/ (accessed January 27-29, 2010).

Padre Pio, "This is your entrance ticket to Heaven" reported of
the Franciscan friar when distributing Holy Face Medals,
http://www.jesusiam.com/pio.html (accessed August 10, 2009)

Pope Benedict XVI, "For Christians, truth has a name: God. And
goodness has a face: Jesus Christ" - excerpted from a discourse to
Czech authorities in Prague, Czech Republic, September 26,
2009,
http://www.zenit.org/article-26969?l=english (accessed
October 5, 2009)

Ratzinger, Cardinal Joseph. "Art and Liturgy - The Question of
Images" *The Spirit of the Liturgy*, 115. San Francisco, USA:
Ignatius Press, 2000.

Reverend Lawrence Farley, p.d., "An Insult To Catholic
Teaching", email response online, September 29, 2009,
https://www.americaneedsfatima.net/campaigns/E0071/fr-
mcbrien-protest.html

Rigamonti, Sister Maria Ildefonsa. *The Story of Sister Maria Pierina
De Micheli.* Milan, Italy: King Bros 1957.

Roman Catholic Church. "Holy Images" *Catechism of the Catholic
Church*, 1159-1162, 1192. Libera Editriice Vaticana, Citta del
Vaticano 1993.

Roman Catholic Church. "Popular Piety" *Catechism of the Catholic Church*, 1164-1179. Libera Editriice Vaticana, Citta del Vaticano, 1993.

"One development of far-reaching importance in the history of the images of faith was the emergence for the first time of a so-called *acheiropoietos*, an image that has not been made by human hands and portrays the very face of Christ. Two of these images appeared in the East at about the same time in the middle of the sixth century. The first of these was the so-called camulianium, the imprint of the image of Christ on a woman's gown. The second was the mandylion, as it was called later, which was brought from Edessa in Syria to Constantinople and is thought by many scholars today to be identical with the Shroud of Turin. In each case, as with the Turin Shroud, it must have been a question of a truly mysterious image, which no human artistry was capable of producing. In some inexplicable way, it appeared imprinted upon cloth and claimed to show the true face of Christ, the crucified and risen Lord. The first appearance of this image must have provoked immense fascination. Now at last could the true face of the Lord, hitherto hidden, be seen and thus the promise be fulfilled: *"He who has seen me has seen the Father"* (Jn 14:9).

– Cardinal Joseph Ratzinger, *"Art and Liturgy - The Question of Images"*, in his book *"The Spirit of the Liturgy"*, 2000

www.transnumerique.com